Winning Pr
And Personally

How to Use Easy and Successful Skills to Dramatically Improve Your Leadership, Team building and Communication With Groups and Individuals

Air

Fire

Water

Earth

Shay Thoelke and Stefan Neilson
Winning Colors® Adult Series Volume I

Winning Professionally and Personally

How To Use Easy and Successful Skills to Dramatically Improve Your Leadership, team Building and Communication with Groups and Individuals
Adult Series Volume I

Vintage First Edition
Solid Platinum
Published by Aeon Hierophant.
P. O. Box 7276, Seattle WA 98043

Text and Art copyright © 1999 Stefan & Shay   Art by Shay Thoelke
The material content of this text is based upon the concept and theory of a present behavioral communication identification process called Winning Colors® by Stefan Neilson. All rights reserved. No part of this book, including written material and illustrations, may be reproduced or transmitted in any form or by any means, electronic or mechanical, including photocopying, recording or by any information storage and retrieval system without the permission in writing from the author, except by a reviewer who wishes to quote brief passages in connection with a review written for inclusion in a magazine or newspaper.

Edited by Rich Thoelke and Leilani Thoelke
ISBN 1-880830-53-1
Printed in the United States of America
Distributed by Aeon Communications, Inc.
The Winning Colors® series:
Color Me Rich, Color Me Wealthy
© 1981 Stefan ISBN 0-9606110-0-2
Personality Language , Revised Edition © 1982 Stefan & Shay
Here's Looking at You, Kid © 1990, 1992 Stefan & Shay
Energizing: The Internet of the Brain © 1997 Rich and Shay
Careers Unlimited "To Be or Not to Be! " © 1999
Conflict Resolution Through Winning Colors© 1999
Elementary, Teen, High School Manuals for Instructors and Participants

For information write or call:

Aeon Communications, Inc.
18021 Fremont Ave. N.
Seattle WA 98133

Aeon Communications, Inc.
P. O. Box 96
Mountlake Terrace WA 98043

Aeon Communications, Inc.
Thunderbird Estates, P. O. Box
Harrison Hot Springs, B.C. VOM 1K0
Canada

Aeon Communications, Inc.
P. O. Box 7276
Seattle, WA 98133
USA
(425) 672-8222 fax (425) 672-9777

e-mail: winningcolors@mindspring.com

Dedicated to Rich Thoelke

Your written contributions and ideas are not documented in this text but they are entwined throughout the pages. You are an integral part of Winning Colors ®.

Thank you friend.

About the Authors:

Shay Thoelke is a graduate of the University of Washington. She completed her MA in Integrated Curriculum from City University and has written multiple curricula for schools. Her thirty years of instruction include Martha Washington State Institution, Echo Glen State School for Girls and Boys, junior high school with Seattle Public Schools and senior high with Edmonds Public Schools. In addition she has done extensive seminars and workshops for business, education and the military throughout the USA and Canada. Her public services have been consistently reported and interviewed in the media. In 1985 she was chosen Teacher of the Year for the Edmonds School District. From 1979 to 1995 she was honored by the graduating senior classes. She was selected by Who's Who in America's Teachers in 1994. In 1995 Shay became the recipient of the Excellence in Education Christie McAuliffe Award: "In recognition of outstanding contribution to the education and support of Washington State students." She has written <u>Energizing the Internet of the Brain</u> and a book of haiku poetry <u>Thoughts of the Seasons: A Journey Through the Colors</u>. Her most recent contributions include three volumes focusing on <u>Service Learning A Team Community Experience</u> in the middle school and high school.

Stefan Neilson was graduated in psychology with an MA from Columbia University, New York. As an author, instructor of upper management and university professor, Stefan uses his twelve years of university training as a consultant, seminar and convention director. His expertise includes consulting, communication, keynotes, counseling, teaching, radio and television interviews. Seminars and keynotes have included such clients as McDonald's National Management Association, General Dynamics, JROTC and various school districts throughout the nation. Stefan was director of Counseling and Guidance for a dozen high schools and is presently the president of Aeon Communications. Over 150,000 students in 1600 schools have participated up to the present in the Winning Colors® process. His corporate, business and educational seminar participants have applauded his new dynamic, hands-on, practical and innovative approach.

Together Stefan and Shay combine depth of knowledge and experience in business, education, consultation and counseling in presenting hands-on seminars and innovative, bottom-line communication workbooks and texts. Their dynamic and caring presentations provide you with keynotes, seminars and cost/time effective materials that you will remember, value and use.

Contents

Origins of Western Thought	2
Four Ingredients for a Successful Career	3
People Have Different Learning Styles	4
Step #1 Begin by Identifying Communications Strengths	5
How to Begin	6
Discover Form	7
Scoring Your **Winning Colors**®	8
Win! Win! Win!	9
The Sum of Our Parts	10
Your **Winning Colors**® Secrets	11
I Have an Emotional Attachment	13
Expand Your Awareness	15
Step #2 Assess the Behavioral Predominance of Any Person or Situation	17
Color Me Observing	18
Step #3 Personal Empowerment Statements	19
Step #4 Secret Personality Form	23
My People Watcher's List	26
Step #5 The Four Parts of Self	29
The Planner Part of Me	31
The Adult Planner in Summary	62
Planner Communication Key	70
The Builder Part of Me	71
How Do You Make Decisions?	83
The Decision Making Process	86
The Adult Builder in Summary	99
Builder Communication Key	107
The Relater Part of Me	109
The Adult Relater in Summary	137
Relater Communication Key	147
The Adventurer Part of Me	149
The Adult Adventurer in Summary	177
Adventurer Communication Key	188
Hot Button Value	189
A Bad Dream or a Nightmare?	191
So How Do You Deal With a Bad Dream or Nightmare in the Form of a Leader?	194
Journaling Form	198
On a Personal Level	199
A Time to Follow, A Time to Lead, A Time to be Interdependent	204
Power Chart	205

Notes from the Author

As adults we know growth, educationally, professionally and personally must be a life-long on-going process. It is like dropping a pebble in the center of a pool of water. The rings form and begin rippling across the pond of our life. Like the rings on our pond, as we move through this process we are continually evolving. We are gatherers. We are readers. We are accessing the informational highway. We are involved in training programs and seminars. New people entering our lives are impacting us. Others are leaving our circle. Our daily life experiences are adding new rings in our pond. And along the way, there are those great "A-Ha!" moments. What is motivating us today may not motivate us tomorrow. As our focuses shift or change so do our behavioral motivations. These shifts may require that we bring up another color strength be it Planner, Builder, Relater or Adventurer.

The next step is to assess if you have successfully developed the color you chose to focus upon.

This can be done by:
Resorting the cards yourself as explained on page 6

Having your significant other sort the cards according to how he or she sees you

Having a family member, children(children cards , middle school and teen cards are available) sort the cards according to how they see you

Having someone on your management team, a fellow employee or support staff person you trust, sort the cards assessing your progress

Having a friend or family member complete the Secret Identifier list with you as the focus

Remember most limits in life are self-imposed.

Shay

Celebrate your strengths
  Know you are all four colors
    Blue, Green, Brown and Red

        Know you are all four elements
        Air, Water, Earth and Fire
        The circle of life

            Prism of colors
            Change is seeking new paths
            Enjoy the journey
                ---Shay

Winning Professionally and Personally

How to use easy and successful skills to dramatically improve your leadership, team building and communication with groups and individuals

By

Shay Thoelke and Stefan Neilson

The Dance
Of
The Elements

The Planner part seeks to understand the universe and its unknowns. Thoughts like deep green ocean currents are constantly tumbling while seeking innovative and logical outcomes. Detail and planning are essential. For the Planner freedom of thought is deeply valued. Like a harlequin, the Planner wants to dance the dance, but often times will do so behind the anonymity of a mask.

The Relater part seeks harmony in the universe. Like the blue sky, the Relater is open. Humanitarian needs will always find an advocate and a friend in the Relater. Judgments will be made based upon people first and secondly on facts. Emotions are valued as a means of keeping individuals in society from becoming intellectual robots. A romantic at heart, the Relater will organize the dance.

The Builder part seeks to bring order to the universe. Unknowns are to be solved based upon facts. Too much detail clutters. Tradition, commitment and responsibility are roots to be valued and sunken deep into the rich brown earth. Diplomacy, leadership, strength and direction are valued. Life is to be built upon a solid rock foundation. The dance will be danced if it serves a worthwhile purpose.

The Adventurer part chooses to explore the universe and all of its unknown frontiers. The Adventurer's element is found in flames of red in the form of fire. Deprive the fire of open air and the Adventurer's flame will begin to flicker. Challenge and action are fuel to the Adventurer. Neither the result nor the details of the process are significant. Life is a sensual experience. The dance will be danced if it is among the clouds or beneath the seas.

Let the Dance Begin . . .

Two may **talk**
together
under the same roof
for years,
yet **never** really **meet:**
and two others
at **first speech**
are old **friends**

> -Mary Catherwood "Marianson"
> Mackinac and Lake Stories

In order to understand the following pages,
it is absolutely crucial to keep in mind the terms:

Planner, **Builder,** Relater and Adventurer

are abbreviated forms of and always signify:

Planner Part of Self
Builder Part of Self
Relater Part of Self
Adventurer Part of Self

Winning Colors® is a whole person approach[1] based on proven behavioral, client-centered and neurolinguistic research.

The followers of 19th century type theorists hold the belief that a person's personality is built on an innate system which is imprinted with specific ways of thinking, understanding, valuing and conceptualizing.

There is no empirical evidence to substantiate such contentions.
Winning Colors® categorically holds
that there is no such reality as a "personality type!"

---

[1] © Stefan & Shay *Leadership, Team Building, Conflict Resolution, Self-esteem, Communication,* **Page 5, 9-11,** Aeon Hierophant, Seattle WA, 1998

Origins of Western Thought
Two strands of analysis of humankind

Absolute Certainty/Control	Mystery/Dignity of the Person
Hippocrates (460-380 B.C.): father of modern medicine (four types) **Parmenides**: stability **Galen** (Roman, c. 2 A.D.) Types: phlegmatic, choleric, melancholic, sanguine **Absolute Certainty/Control** **Predestination** (c 1500) **Machiavelli** (1469-1527): The Prince **Divine Right of Kings** (c 1600) **Descartes** (1596-1650): matter vs. form **Napoleon** (1852-1882) **Darwin** (1809-1882): survival of the fittest **Phrenology** (c 1850) **Type theory** **Totalitarianism, Fascism, Capitalism** (c 1900) **Nazism** **Assessments**: designed for control/mathematical certainty in analysis of people's thinking, feelings, actions **Jung**: type (introversion, extroversion) **Lorge-Thorndike**: intelligence level slot **Kiersey-Bates** (True Colors), DISC, Performax, et al. type casting **Humankind can be totally controlled, figured out, measured, pigeon-holed and type cast.**	**Socrates** (469-399 B.C.): "Know thyself" **Hericlitus**: change **Plato** (429-347 B.C.): world of forms **Aristotle** (384-347 B.C.): matter and form united Beginning of dignity and personal freedom Democracy Respect for the person developed throughout the first millennium under the influence of Judaism and Christianity **Magna Carta** (1215 A.D.): French and American Revolutions and constitutional changes in England promoted democracy **20th Century** **Einstein**: relativity **Heisenberg**: uncertainty principle Development of various processes based on freedom and respect of the person to change and mature **Behavior Modification**: change is possible **Client-centered Therapy**: person controls change **Rotter's Locus of Control**: change of behavioral focus creates balance **Dune**: differences in learning style **Neurolinguistics**: how words affect people in different ways **Rorschach** testing designs **Winning Colors®**: observation tool designed to assist persons in understanding and dealing practically with present thinking, deciding, feeling and action behaviors. **Persons are free agents, each in control of his/her own destiny**

The Four Ingredients for
Any Successful and Personal Satisfactory Career

- A foundation of general knowledge
- Know-how (specific knowledge required by the job description)
- Physical and mental skills (surgeon, carpenter, basketball player, mathematician)
- Behaviors required as a *prerequisite* for success by the career definition.

The identification, acquiring and matching of crucial personal behaviors to those required by the career description, personal or professional relationships, communication strengths, volunteer community service and successful goal attainment is **seldom if ever given credence!**

You Are Here X

Begin by identifying where you are. Next identify and acquire tools to make that journey a sensational success.

This text is designed to empower you to:

- Identify your present behavioral communication strengths.
- Identify the behaviors required to meet your objectives.
- Give you concrete strategies and exercises for developing behaviors required for being successful and fulfilled in your career choice and communication with others.

People have different learning styles.

Karen Rheault has linked Gardner's research which " . . . suggests that we all possess at least 8 intelligence areas . . ." with ways to exercise and develop them. She states, "Each of us has all of these intelligences, but not all of them are developed equally. Because of this we do not use them effectively. One or two intelligences may be stronger and more fully developed than others. However, this does not need to be a permanent condition. . ." At her Multiple Intelligence home Page http://member.tripod.com/~RheaultK/index.html she makes the connection between "Using Multiple Intelligences To Enhance Learning" and educators in a concise and clear manner. The following listing is taken from her TEACHER TOOLBOX:

🜚 Verbal/Linguistic: reading, biographies, poetry, storytelling, humor/jokes, creative writing, debate, journal writing, explanations, feelings, reports, lists, library research

✵ Logical/Mathematical: analyzing, calculations, classifying, pattern games, time lines, numbers, logic problems, experimentation, critical thinking, sequencing, outlining, compare and contrast, graphic organizers, scientific thinking, venn diagrams, writing problems, reasoning, problem solving.

✺ Visual/Spatial: guided imagery, collages, drawing, designs, posters, mapping, fantasy, imagination, labeling, pictures, pretending.

✿ Body/Kinesthetic: acting, drama, dancing, exercise, physical gestures, experiment, inventing, movement, role playing, human graph, demonstrations, hands-on thinking (manipulatives).

♋ Musical/Rhythmic: chants, rhythmic patterns, listening, rap, singing, music performance, humming, instrumental sounds, music creation.

⌘ Interpersonal: feedback, cooperative groups, discussions, group projects, teamwork, role-playing, person-to-person communication, empathy practices, interviews, team assessment.

✾ Intrapersonal: reflection, autobiography, concentration, focusing, goal setting, self-identification, thinking strategies, higher order reasoning, metacognition, free choice time, awareness of personal feelings.

❖ Naturalist: create observation notebooks, draw natural scenes, photography, describe changes in the environment, binoculars, telescopes, microscopes, magnifiers, classify and categorize things in nature, design venn diagrams.

Where do you fit? What are your present intelligence strengths? What intelligences need developing?

- In order to accommodate those who have a different way of learning and processing information, on page 7 is a pen and pencil approach to discovering behavioral strengths.

- We suggest that both the card sort and written form be used. Compare them and make a decision as to the predominate behaviors as indicated on page 9: Win! Win! Win!

For an in depth study of Learning Styles: I've Got Style, Bud Pues, ISBN 1-880830-49-3

Step #1: Begin Now by Identifying Your Present Behavioral Communication Strengths!

Why is this crucial?

- Behaviors are visible!
- They are concrete!
- You can check them out!

Examples:

Are you decisive or not?   (Have you heard someone say: "Oh, Jim can never make up his mind about anything!")

Do you smile?   (Have you heard someone say: "Joan, you never smile. Don't take life so seriously all the time!")

The next few pages show you how to identify:

- your **present** behaviors and communication strengths

- clusters of your present behavioral preferences

- **present** behaviors, behavioral preference and communication strengths of **any** person

- **present** motivation, self-esteem of both yourself and others

> On the following pages are the tools to identify yours and others' **present** communication strengths in a matter of minutes.

How to Begin

Clockwork green, brown, blue and red!

1. Locate your color cards on the back inside flap cover of the book.

2. Place the four-color cards before you as a clock, illustrations up.
   Place one at the 12 o'clock position, the next at the 3 o'clock position,
   the next at the 6 o'clock position and the last card at the 9 o'clock position.

3. Read the words. Look at the illustrations.

   > Ask yourself this question: Which Card Is Truly Like Me?
   > Which Card Is My Winning Color?

4. Based on your own internal feelings and thoughts
   (not what you think or feel others expect of you),
   rearrange the cards by placing
   the card that best describes you at the 12 o'clock position,
   the next at the 3 o'clock position,
   the next at the 6 o'clock position
   and the least like you at the 9 o'clock position.

5. Assign numbers to the colored cards, based on the ranking you just
   made, with #1 the most like you at the 12 o'clock position,
   #4 the least like you placed at the 9 o'clock position.

   > **READ** the back of the card you chose as #1
   > Is this like you?
   > If not, go through the cards again, making a new choice.

6. Indicate below in which order you sorted your cards (1-4):

   - ☐ *Planner*
   - ☐ **Builder**
   - ☐ Relater
   - ☐ Adventurer

Your Communication DISCOVER Power

Which part of you is the strongest at the present time?
- *Planner?* * **Builder?** * Relater? * Adventurer?

These are the four parts of self.
Number the following words or phrases in each item (a,b,c,d) from 1 to 4, moving horizontally across each line in order of importance to you. Number 1 would be the word or phrase that **best describes your feelings of comfort and what you are like inside - NOT** how you would like **to be - NOT** how you act because of outside pressures, e. g., peers, school, work, superiors, family, friends.
Total the vertical columns.
Circle the lowest score. Put a box around your second lowest score.
The **lowest score** identifies your **present** communication **POWER** or **Winning Color.** Your boxed score is your present back up communication Power.
Read page 8 and then fill in the **TREND** blanks with the four parts of self that match the words in the column.
Next fill in the **COLOR** blanks with the color that matches the **TREND** based on page 8.

a) ☐ Being prepared   b) ☐ Let's all be friends   c) ☐ Developing better and more logical ways   d) ☐ Living today and not worrying about tomorrow

a) ☐ Telling people what they should do   b) ☐ Talking and socializing   c) ☐ Understanding and analyzing about tomorrow   d) ☐ Having fun and excitement with friends

a) ☐ Saving and budgeting   b) ☐ Giving   c) ☐ Creating   d) ☐ Spending

a) ☐ Leading   b) ☐ Relating   c) ☐ Planning   d) ☐ Exploring

a) ☐ Being organized   b) ☐ Being loved and accepted   c) ☐ Being correct and competent   d) ☐ Being in spontaneous action

Total:
____   ____   ____   ____

Trend:
____   ____   ____   ____

Color:
____   ____   ____   ____

Scoring Your Winning Colors®
DANGER! DANGER! DANGER!

This may have been the first time you have looked at the good things about yourself. You may not be sure, at first, which word fits you. You may not be sure whether your strength is * Planner? * **Builder?** * Relater? * Adventurer? This is okay. On page 7 you were to put down what you believe now! As you discover more about yourself, you may want to change your choice. **Change your answer whenever you have new insights.**

Remember, there is no right or wrong choice. You may discover other people have told you things about yourself that do not fit.

NOW you are discovering what is good about you!

STEP # 1:
Under column a) the TREND is **Builder** and the COLOR is **BROWN.**
Under column b) the TREND is Relater and the COLOR is **BLUE.**
Under column c) the TREND is Planner and the COLOR is **GREEN**
Under column d) the TREND is Adventurer and the COLOR is **RED.**

STEP # 2: Fill in the appropriate trend word and corresponding color

STEP #3: What the colors represent

Under column a) the COLOR is **BROWN** like the earth and shows leadership and decisiveness.
Under column b) the COLOR is **BLUE** and reflects the sky, showing openness and feeling.
Under column c) the COLOR is **GREEN** like the ocean with deep, hidden, changing currents.
Under column d) the COLOR is **RED** and reflects fire, shows excitement, action and fun.

The **Four Elements of Life:**

    Earth
    Air
    Water
    Fire

WIN! WIN! WIN!

Place your choices (in pencil) for the color cards and discover form below.

Color card	**Discover form**

Number 1 to 4 below:　　　　　　　　　　Place your scores in the first blank, then
(12 o'clock is your # 1 card, etc.)　　　　number 1 to 4, (#1 is your lowest score)

Green card (*Planner*) ____	____ ____ *Planner* (green)
Brown card (**Builder**) ____	____ ____ **Builder** (brown)
Blue card (Relater) ____	____ ____ Relater (blue)
Red card (Adventurer) ____	____ ____ Adventurer (red)

Compare the two sets. If there is a difference, pick the one you think is closest to the true you. Remember, you may change your choice any time you discover more about your true self. Your second choice is very important, too. This is your backup strength.

I am proud of the true me!

Place your final choice below in pencil so you may erase it if you discover something new about how you truly are inside. You will be able to remove the mask!
Number from 1- 4 the final way I see myself for the present is:

☐ *Planner* (green)　　　　　　　　　☐ **Builder** (brown)
☐ Relater (blue)　　　　　　　　　　☐ Adventurer (red)

Review of your card sorting exercise
Your Challenge
It is important for you to remember that no matter how you sorted the cards, you are made up of all four colors.

The goal of **Winning Colors®** is to seek a balance of all four colors. There will be times when, in different situations, you may choose to exercise one color more strongly than another. For example, in some work situations the **brown behaviors** are important. What you don't want to do is turn into Garfield, a cartoon cat, who is totally brown and regularly beats up on his master, John, and his housemate dog.

In social situations with friends and family, you may choose to exhibit your **blue behaviors** and, like Ziggy, find the rainbows in life's relationships. When detail and thoughtful consideration are needed in a situation, emphasize your **green behaviors**. But, once again, don't turn into a cartoon Cathy, a Planner/Relater, who is so burdened by guilt and the fear of making a wrong decision that she makes no decision. When you need adventure and fun in life, present Snoopy's **red behaviors** as he puts on his goggles, helmet and scarf and takes to the skies as the Red Baron Von Richthofen.

THE SUM OF OUR PARTS

Each of us has a personality with these identifiable parts. The dominant ones guide our behavior in any given situation. These are our strengths. Other people's strengths will be different and can cause communication problems. When we can recognize this, we are more effective in our communications.

Builders focus on the desired result. They are not interested in exploring details. They want a concise plan, preferably in outline fashion and above all, as brief as possible. It should be organized chronologically step-by-step with clarity and focus on the goal. The **Builder** values accountability, respect, preparation, tradition and rules. In keeping with these values, they save, invest and strive for financial success. Status symbols are most important to **Builders** and serve as evidence of achievement. They want to run things their way. **Builders** have little consideration for either the social nature of **Relaters**, or the lighthearted and spontaneous nature of **Adventurers**. They are impatient with **Planners** who investigate everything thoroughly before completing the project. The **Builder** wants to get to the "results" quickly.

Relaters focus on people. Relationships are primary, whatever the project or goal. They make others feel needed and valued, either intentionally or as a by-product of their interest. **Relaters** join groups of all kinds and work within the group to keep it harmonious. They possess a remarkable eye for exterior detail. Strangers will befriend the **Relater**. They are warm, giving and generous. Credit the **Relaters** in corporations for creating some sense of a "family" atmosphere. They are the glue of human contact. They are team builders. The actions of **Relaters** are emotion based. Other personalities think of **Relaters** as nonessential. Both **Builders** and **Planners** may think the **Relater** wastes time on feelings. However, reflect on a world without caregivers and the relevance of **Relaters** is obvious.

Planners **epitomize the idea of the internal thinker**. The goal can only be reached by a thorough examination of all details of the process. Deadlines are burdensome since the completion of the examination process may take more time than allowed. The internal analyzing of ideas goes hand-in-hand with planning, budgeting, innovative and logical thought. As a result of this motivation, **Planners** are exceedingly creative. They are content to work independently and will avoid distractions. With their focus on the thorough examination of possibilities, they are considered too serious by other personalities. **Planners** are, however, invaluable to the successful completion of any project because they invest whatever time and effort is necessary to cover all options before making a decision or reaching a goal.

Adventurers are action focused and live in the present. Spontaneity is natural. Excitement is their lifeblood. Some measure of risk is most often a requirement. They thrive on challenge. If forced to just sit, their brains go into the "park" mode. **Adventurers** will get things done with little waste of time and have a dislike for any structure or routine. The **Adventurer** creates fun in an otherwise boring process. **Adventurers** don't understand the motivation of the **Builders** or **Planners**, believing both to be too serious and intense. The **Adventurer** believes the **Relaters** are too focused on people and lack excitement. **Adventurers** are often undervalued by other personalities as frivolous and not very serious but we often live vicariously through them. They are the natural entrepreneurs, following a star they create.

Your **Winning Colors**® *secrets*

The secret of **Winning Colors®** is that it shows you how to identify the four parts of self. Unfortunately, whether by upbringing or choice, most people develop a bias to a certain behavioral pattern. This bias is due to the *Planner*, **Builder,** Relater or ADVENTURER part of self.

Winning Colors® allows you to examine these biases objectively. It gives you strategies for dealing effectively with people who demonstrate a certain behavioral attachment. In the process, you develop the other parts of self as you identify and bring up those behaviors necessary for present moment successful communication.

When using **Winning Colors®**, it is crucial that you are both aware of, and follow, these rules of thumb:
1) **Winning Colors®** indicates the **PRESENT BEHAVIORS** of self and others.
2) With this behavioral self-awareness, a person has personal communication strength know-how. **Winning Colors®** is based on the prudential process (doing the right thing at the right time). The first function of a wise person is to put things in order. Virtue and strength stand in balance!

> **THINK!** (Planner-Green) My strength is in my ability **to think things through.**
> **DECIDE!** (Builder-Brown) My strength is in my ability **to decide/bottom line it.**
> **FEEL!** (Relater-Blue) My strength lies in my ability **to feel.**
> **ACT!** (Adventurer-Red) My strength is my ability **to take action quickly.**

3) With a knowledge of **present** behaviors, you may choose to reinforce existing behaviors or develop new ones according to your personal goals. **Note the word present!**

It is as if you were to assess your **present** English vocabulary and say you could never learn any new words. You would always have just your present knowledge of English words. But you know better. It is possible to learn new words and expand your vocabulary for the rest of your life. Also, you may expand and develop new behaviors whether they are focused on thinking, feeling, deciding or acting.

Winning Colors® simply assists people:

1) in identifying their invested behaviors (Comfort Zone),
2) in appreciating equally the valuable behaviors of others,
3) in acquiring and developing newly identified behaviors that would be beneficial as a "human becoming".

How to check out the present proportion of your behavioral strengths.

There are four major **clusters of behavior**. In order to remember and quickly put a specific behavior into practice, memory hooks of four words and four colors are used. According to learning styles, some will find color easier to remember and others will recall the descriptive words.

- Those behaviors which cluster around the **thinking part of self**.
  (*Planner* Part of Self: Green)
  Behavioral examples: Thinking, creating, conceptualizing, dreaming, reasoning

- Those behaviors which cluster around the **leader/decision making part of self**.
  (**Builder** Part of Self: Brown)
  Behavioral examples: Leading, deciding, dominating (power), duty oriented, responsible

- Those behaviors which cluster around the **team/emotional part of self**.
  (Relater Part of Self: Blue)
  Behavioral examples: Team-oriented, friendly, giving, talking, loving

- Those behaviors which cluster around the **action part of self**.
  (Adventurer Part of Self: Red)
  Behavioral examples: Doing, performing, risking, playful, fun loving

Take four colored pieces of paper (Green, Brown, Blue and Red). Place them as was done with the cards in a clock formation according to strengths.

Now place them in proportion to behavioral strengths. This will give a present image of the proportion of behavioral strengths. Use removable magic tape to join the sheets together.

Note how, in this case, the behavioral cluster at the 12 o'clock position is stronger than the three o'clock position and so on. What if a chosen career demands 9 o'clock behaviors at the 12 o'clock position? This happens often. For example, consider receptionists who lack **Relater** behaviors. Their blue card would be at the nine o'clock position yet the job demands **Relater** behaviors at the 12 o'clock position. In corporations it often happens that persons lacking behaviors required by the job description are promoted to that position. This is one of the bases for the Peter Principle: the person rises to the top of his/her incompetence.

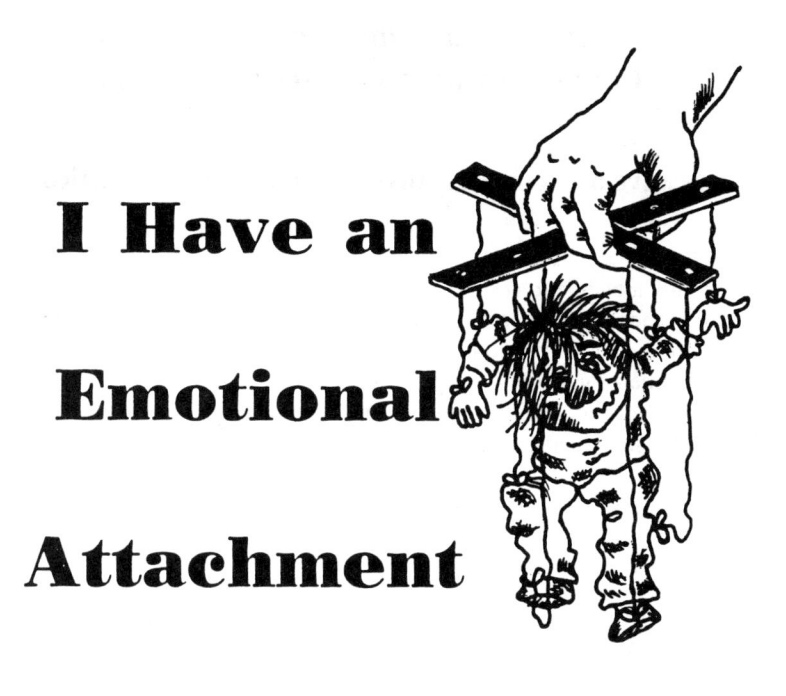

I Have an Emotional Attachment to That to Which I Am First Exposed!

You have an emotional attachment
to that to which you are first exposed!

In order to resolve any conflict, present behavioral identification is crucial!

This means:
You are emotionally attached to certain behaviors.
You usually prefer those people or things you first contact or behaviors you adapt through life.
This is true even in negative situations such as abuse.
A person may become attached to hitting or wanting to be hit.
The first step in any conflict resolution is present behavioral identification.
The following exercise indicates a few of your emotional attachments.

Put a check (✓) by what you like or prefer most:

___ potatoes	___ rice
___ expressing feelings	___ keeping feelings inside
___ classical music	___ country music
___ being in charge	___ being part of the group
___ joking and being on stage	___ serious and reserved
___ thinking	___ action

person #1 (name): _____   or person #2 (name): _____

The behaviors you choose indicate your comfort zone. The basis of conflict is when your comfort zone conflicts with another's.

It is not negative to be attached. Attachment is part of the human condition. Attachment indicates value systems. The crucial fact for success is to recognize the differences between your system of values and those of others.

Winning Colors® is a powerful tool that helps you identify present bias. This attachment may change according to time, circumstances and place. Most communication programs and many personality assessments ignore this! Because you are attached to certain behaviors, you may not even like or respect people who are attached to behaviors unlike your own. This may prevent you from getting along with some people.

**THESE ATTACHMENTS ARE NOT INNATE.
YOU ARE NOT BORN A CERTAIN "TYPE".**

Winning Colors® helps you begin to see that even though something is not important for you, it may be vital to someone else. Both are okay. Your Challenge: Change your colored glasses!
Differences and variety make this world a wonderful place.

Expand Your Awareness and Experience
Your Tremendous Edge for Success

Your **Winning Colors®** gives you **a tremendous edge** in getting along with others and reaching your personal and business goals. **Winning Colors®** helps you get what you want and communicate successfully with anyone whether it is your superiors, peers or family.

Life has many comparisons. In baseball, a batting average is computed by the number of times a player goes up to bat and the number of times he or she hits the ball. If a player hits the ball two times out of every ten, he or she will have a .200 batting average. If that player hits the ball three times out every ten, he or she will have a .300 batting average and hundreds of thousands of dollars more. The baseball player with a .300 batting average hits the ball only one more time out of every ten times up at bat! What a **colossal edge**! **Winning Colors®** shows you how to capture a **tremendous edge** in any communication and reach your goal.

You may have had difficulty understanding other people's ideas and feelings because they act so differently from you. For example, some people like to talk and visit. Others prefer to be silent and think. Some like to get up in front of the group and act very funny. While others like to be in charge and lead. Of course, the mature person can do all four, but most people have a preference.

Good communication skills and a strategy for attaining your goals, whether they be personal riches or financial success, is:

- **Awareness.** When you are capable of deciphering the differences between ideas and feelings of others and your own.

- **A plan of action.** When you have a method for identifying and developing skills and behaviors crucial for communicating with those using different words, ideas and emotions than you.

- **Improved performance.** The result is you know yourself and others better. You are happier, a better leader, liked by more people, successful and have a lot more fun.
  (See the diagram on the next page.)

Awareness Diagram

AWARENESS
Identify my behavioral strengths & how they impact my working style

PLAN OF ACTION

Assess how I am relating to my peers, family, team or co-workers

Assess my peers, family members, team members or co-workers

Develop strategies to meet the 4 clusters of behavior

Help peers, family, team members or co-workers recognize the value of mixing behavioral strengths in cooperative situations

IMPROVED PERFORMANCE

More effective communication with peers, family members, team members, co-workers and or customers

Less stress

Fewer conflicts

Step #2

You are now ready to assess the behavioral predominance of any person or situation.

Color Me Observing

Many people say they know the best way to make friends and get along with people . . . but do they? Do you? Start with persons you think you know.
Prove that you know what motivates and contributes to the self-esteem of others!

Although a person is all four parts, many times certain behavioral clusters are more prominent. How good are you at identifying the best way to communicate? What kind of leader are you? A successful leader knows the behavioral strengths of others.
Guess the **Winning Colors**® of anyone you know . . . superiors, peers, clients, customers, instructors, friends or family!

Name	Brown **Builder**	Blue Relater	Green *Planner*	Red Aðventurer	Score
_____	_____	_____	_____	_____	
Actual Sort	_____	_____	_____	_____	_____
_____	_____	_____	_____	_____	
Actual Sort	_____	_____	_____	_____	_____
_____	_____	_____	_____	_____	
Actual Sort	_____	_____	_____	_____	_____

1. Place the names of the persons you are guessing in the blank space under "name" and above "actual sort."
2. Blank spaces after name: Write the order of the cards after the "name" in the blank spaces (number them 1 to 4 as you think each person will arrange them).
3. Reality check: Have each person arrange the cards as she or he truly feels. Number them from 1 to 4. Place numbered arrangement next to "actual sort."
4. Compare your guess with the actual arrangement of each person's cards.

Score: The more balanced the person, the more difficult it is to choose the order.
5 points if you guess their 1st choice. 4 points if you guess their 2nd choice.
You score 4 points, if their 1st and 2nd choices were the inverse of your choices. Many times the first two behavioral clusters are interchangeable. The backup is very important. Give yourself one point each time you guess their 3rd and 4th choice. It takes practice to pick out the third and fourth cluster. It is not crucial that you do this in the beginning stages.
It is helpful to know the fourth cluster. This indicates the person's behavioral weaknesses and steps may be taken to improve them, if desired.

Total possible score for each person is 11 POINTS.

Number in my group: ____ x 11 = Possible score: ____ My score: ____

Step #3

Personal empowerment statements . . .
How you acquire new behaviors and strengthen present behaviors and skills.

Here is how you do it!

You review the words which describe the *Planner,* **Builder,** Relater or Adventurer behavioral part of you. Choose a desired behavior and build a powerful, positive, empowering assertion of what you want.

Example: (My behavior is nervousness when speaking to a group).
"I choose to stand up in front of a group, say what I want clearly, quickly and with great confidence. It feels great!"

Another example: "I feel a sense of power and am calm and cool when I stand up in front of a group to speak."

You put such personal positive statements on a blank index card. (No lines on card and print clearly).

- **Repeat** the assertion: I **picture** myself in the front of a group speaking as the above personal empowering assertion and **feel** inside myself the power and pleasure of doing it and succeeding.

- **Repeat** each assertion in the morning when you get up and in the evening before going to bed: Think it! See it as a completed fact! Feel it! Key it in with a body signal.

- **Key-in** by associating the personal empowering assertion with a body signal such as touching your thumb and forefinger together as you repeat the assertion. If you key-in strongly enough, you give your subconscious the power to control your body with this signal. You now acquire the successful feeling any time you desire.

Why does this work? When you practice doing an **action correctly** in the imagination and record it in your body memory, **it is like doing it.** The more you practice behaviors, skills and what you want in this way, the easier it will happen.

Crucial: On the following pages, we have designed model personal empowerment statements that may be adapted to your particular need and situation. In each of the following sections, several behaviors and strategies for developing **Planner, Builder, Relater** and **Adventurer** behaviors will be listed. A model affirmation is given which you are encouraged to rework.

The above is adapted from *Color Me Succeeding - Changing* ©1988 Stefan.

Model Personal Empowerment Statements

Customize the following **Personal Empowerment Statements** to your particular goals, needs and circumstances, i.e., "I have a sense of perfection in successfully communicating with (name person or situation) who has strong **Planner** behaviors."

Change general statements to concrete specific statements: "I proceed in a thoughtful and detailed manner," to "I have a sense of perfection in successfully communicating with my **Planner** Instructor/Boss Jim or Client Mary in a thoughtful and detailed manner." Substitute the emotional words that have pay value and meaning for you, i.e., **Builder,** I have a sense of power, security, etc.; **Relater,** I have a warm feeling, sense of honesty, integrity, etc.; **Planner,** I have a sense of perfection, the ability to improve, to predict, to understand etc.; **Adventurer,** I enjoy the thrill, action, fun, excitement, adventure, etc.

Universal statements have little change power. The brain requires concrete visualizations in order to be activated. Whenever possible include a name of the person or group of people involved as well as describing the concrete situation as clearly as possible.

Personal Planner Empowerment Statements.

- My Planner behaviors enable me to gather the details of a situation (name it) so that I may act with success and confidence.
- My keen vision and thoughtful considerations enable me to discover new and better ways of doing (name it).
- I find it a challenge to search out and find out what makes (name) and things (specify) tick. I am trustworthy and faithful to my word with (name or specify situation).
- I enjoy listening and picking up the underlying messages (name person(s) sends.
- I have a sense of power and awe when I think of the mysteries (name) of the Universe.
- I am an excellent listener, have an understanding ear and am capable of a genuine empathy with (name).
- My **Planner** behaviors enable me to plan, predict and explain situations (specify) so that I take the best action path available to me.
- My imagination is strong, creative and vivid in (name situation).
- I am fully aware of the inner needs of those (names) who follow me.
- I enjoy and find it a challenge to be a "possibility thinker" particularly in (name circumstances).
- I have a sense of pride and excitement in performing my job with perfection.
- Developing a plan of action for better team performance or a sale presentation is easy and simple for me.
- I enter into serious conversations with others in an easy and interesting manner.
- I look before I leap (specify situation or person).

Personal Builder Empowerment Statements.
- I am quickly aware of the practical steps to take in organizing my life for financial success.
- I have a deep sense of confidence as a practical **Builder** who bottom lines with ease (name situation or person). I am able to give a clear outline of what I want (name situation or with name the person).
- I enjoy presenting my requests (name them and to whom) in an organized step-by-step fashion.
- I have a sense of power and self-confidence and am able to arm wrestle successfully with fellow **Builders** (name them).
- I deal with the traditional values and traditions of **Builders** (name) with confidence and ease.
- Regardless of the odds, I can take any **Builder** (name) on and have the power to endure until I win.
- My home, work, game or exam is number one. I am the greatest! I am number one.
- When I act, I get the result (name it) I want.
- I have a sense of pride in being decisive in (name the situation) or with (name the person).
- I am electric, setting up an atmosphere of respect and charisma (name situation).
- As the Rock of Gibraltar, temporary setbacks only increase my passionate drive toward successfully achieving my goal (indicate goal).
- As a powerful **Builder** leader, I take the first action step (name situation) or begin conversations in a strong forceful manner as required.
- I enjoy being faithful, vigilant, steadfast and committed to tasks I choose to undertake.
- I respect others for their endurance and courage.

Personal Relater Empowerment Statements.
- I enjoy and find it a challenge in being a people-centered person (name situation or with whom).
- I enjoy taking the time to help (name those in need).
- Feelings are important to me. I express them easily to (name or situation).
- I control my feelings by checking out the thoughts that started them (name person or situation).
- I am a positive person creating harmony in stressful situations (name).
- I take pride in relating in an honest and open manner to (name).
- My sparkling cheerfulness and friendly company makes (name) enjoy being around me.
- My Relater senses are extremely active picking up the exterior details of situations (name) with ease.
- I reveal my inner life with ease to (name person or in situations) when I choose.
- I find it easy and enjoyable to associate with strangers. Within minutes they are comfortable and are strangers no more (name situation).
- I take pride in being able to pick up on exterior details (name the situation).
- It is easy for me to make people(name of person or situation) feel good about themselves.
- I am a strong, sensitive leader and lead my team (name) with personal concern to success and profit.
- I am a warm, gentle and gracious person to all I meet (name situations).
- I enjoy and feel comfortable wearing a warm smile when meeting people (name situations).

Personal Adventurer Empowerment Statements.
- I thrill at the excitement and action of the game (name).
- I take tiredness, hunger and pain in my stride as I climb to the top (name).
- I enjoy living the present moment to the fullest.
- Change and travel are my middle name.
- I am a fun person to be with at all times.
- I enjoy the thrill of taking a chance (name person or situation) and riding the trapeze of life successfully.
- Work is fun (name it). I chose to do what I want to do (name) with confidence and personal satisfaction.
- I enjoy joining in the celebration of life. I relax easily (name situation).
- I share my possessions and abilities with my fellow humans (name) as required within my capabilities.
- I take time to enjoy the pleasures (specify) my senses stir within.
- I control and have a sense of power over the machines (name and describe) I operate.
- I sense machines (name) as an extension of myself so as to utilize them fully in my daily life.
- I have mechanical ability (name situation and machine involved) and machines respond to my wishes immediately.
- I live and thrive on the here and now.
- I find it easy to be lighthearted, join in and create laughter around me (name situation).
- I am an easygoing, fun person to be with at home, work or play (specify).
- I not only seek out the end of the rainbow, but jump over it! (specify)

Step #4

Reality Check Secret Personality Form

How to check your progress in developing new Winning Colors®

This identification process positively reveals the individual as a complete personality with trends toward certain developed behaviors. These behaviors, in turn, prompt actions/reactions and, therefore, are predictable. Recognizing the trends of others using the same process allows for the change in behavior to accommodate communication between individuals.

It is important to remember that the raw scores may change somewhat in different situations. The relationship between the scores will probably remain the same, continuing to reflect the same strengths and weaknesses in different situations.

The object is to become aware that your personality strengths guide your behaviors. Other people have different strengths. Recognizing the differences is the key to communicating effectively.

We may improve communication in two ways:

1. Become aware of our own personality weaknesses and work on them to improve communication with others.

2. Recognize and draw on the differing strengths of others to compliment our weakness.

How to use Your *Winning Colors*® Communication Evaluation Tools

1) Evaluation tools: **Secret Personality Identifier List** and **Discover Form.**

2) What is the **Secret Personality Identifier List**? It is a list of positive behavioral action words. All are beneficial. One is not better than another!

3) First complete the form for yourself on page 25.

4) Next select as many persons as possible who seem to you to have very different behavioral clusters and who:

a) have authority over you   b) are under your authority   c) are peers or friends

If a) or b) is not relevant to your situation, then increase the c) category. For a valid assessment of your communication strengths you should have at least ten persons of each cluster (**Planner, Builder, Relater, Adventurer**) for your sample. The more people involved the better.

5) Have the persons fill out the **Discover Form** or **Sort the Cards** in order to identify persons from each cluster.

6) Ask them to check the words in the **Secret Personality Identifier List** which apply to you. Ask them to indicate the behaviors they personally see in you. Ask them to be as candid as possible. There are no right or wrong answers. You want their truthful assessment of your visible behavioral communications strengths. All are positive. There is no possible insult.

7) **Why is it "secret?"** Fill out the form according to the behaviors you think/feel you have. You do not show it to anyone. Find others who are strong in either **Planner, Builder, Relater, Adventurer** behaviors. Have them check off the list of behaviors which they have seen you demonstrate. You then compare their assessment and yours. How does it check out? This is a reality check.

8) Note the differences of how persons having different groupings of the four clusters experience your communication.

9) Identify the qualities you wish to acquire. Use the methods in the *Winning Colors*® process to help you. You may wish to develop certain parts of self.

10) Two months after you have worked on developing your communication strengths, have the same persons check the **Secret Personality Identifier List** again about you. For example, if you have worked on your **Builder** behaviors and **Builders** have checked the form; are there a greater number of **Builder** behaviors checked off?

11) Evaluate your progress by comparing the pre- and post-evaluations.

12) These are a few of the benefits to be gained:
The tools for dealing with anyone effectively, a powerful leadership style and team building skills.

Secret Personality Identifier List

Check **every** word description that suits either *yourself* or the *behavior* of *the person whom you wish to* identify.

Remember that you are identifying clusters of learned behavior, not pigeonholing the person. Behaviors may change.

Total each column: The highest total indicates the strongest communication strength of the person, as perceived by the observer.

Secret Personality Identifier List

♠ BUILDER	♥ RELATER	♣ PLANNER	♦ ADVENTURER
__ prepared	__ friendly	__ logical	__ playful
__ saves	__ gives	__ creative	__ spends
__ leader	__ relater	__ strategist	__ mover
__ being in control	__ being accepted	__ being perfect	__ being spontaneous
__ dutiful	__ romantic	__ independent	__ comradeship
__ sensible	__ harmonious	__ theoretical	__ lighthearted
__ responsible	__ loving	__ skeptical	__ exciting
__ power	__ sensitive heart	__ predicts	__ complete freedom
__ law and order	__ emotional	__ thinker	__ action
__ dependable	__ sympathetic	__ exactness	__ risks and chance
__ status	__ honest feelings	__ reasonable	__ fun and games
__ track record	__ people-centered	__ analyzing	__ fast machines
__ authority	__ exterior detail	__ interior detail	__ quick
__ tradition	__ act as a team	__ innovative	__ merry making
__ accountable	__ group projects	__ mastery	__ easycome, easygo

Total checks: ♠ Builder ____ ♥ Relater ____ ♣ Planner ____ ♦ Adventurer ____

1985, 1998 Stefan & Shay P. O. Box 7276, Seattle WA 98133.

My People Watcher's List

Become acquainted with all people, who are important to your success, whether they are your subordinates, equals or superiors. Each person you meet should be a subject for close study. Each person's general appearance, speech pattern and walk will give you valuable clues as to his/her **Winning Colors®**. Your goal is to pick out the major champion trend of any person soon after meeting him/her. The following action plan is designed to do just that: to delegate this perceptive skill to the automatic realm of your subconscious.

Just as you practice the proper stroking pattern in order to become a good golfer, you need to practice people watching skills in order to become a good communicator. This people watching exercise will empower you to enter the world of real people in an effective, efficient and loving manner.

For the next two weeks, proceed methodically with each person you wish to remember:

1) Memorize the person's name with its correct spelling. Repeat it several times in the conversation. Associate the particular grade, position, job, phone and address if applicable.
2) Guess his/her age, height and weight. Compare it with yours.
3) Examine the head in detail. Note the style of hair, shape of forehead, eyes, nose, mouth, ears and hair color.
4) Observe the texture and shape of the hands and nails.
5) Take account of the color and style of clothes. What is the condition of the clothes? Are the clothes tidy, worn, or tasteful?
6) Note the use of makeup or glasses.
7) Observe the body language such as repeated movements. Are there any particular gestures?
8) Study the walk. Direct your attention to the sound of his/her steps so that you might identify the individual again. A good exercise is to identify a person **by the sound of his/her steps** as he/she approaches you. You may always check to see if you were correct.
9) Study the voice: accent, inflections, repeated phrases, tone change (one-to-one basis, in-groups, with males, females).
10) Guess the behavioral strengths: **Planner, Builder, Relater, Adventurer**. Give the reasons.
11) Check out your assessment with the card sort or discover form.

    Sample: **People Watcher's Form**

1) **Name:** Jan Michael, President, Success Unlimited Club, (213) 777-7777 4560 Wilshire Blvd. Los Angeles, CA 99046
2) **Age:** 16 years (approximately my age). **Height-Weight:** 6 feet, 180 lbs. (4" taller & 20 lbs. heavier than I)
3) **Head - Hair:** parted on one side and combed over to the left, brown
   Forehead: long, tends to bulge out, **eyes:** squints a lot, blue, **nose:** big (Pinnochio type)
   Lips: full, a bit large, **ears:** Normal looking, neither flat nor protruding
4) **Hands:** smooth, no manual labor, long fingers, wears a ring
5) **Clothes:** dull colors, blue, conservative
6) **Glasses and makeup:** I think he wears contacts
7) **Body Language:** movements are few, steeples hands when making a point, is an overpowering presence in a group, strong hand shake
8) **Walk:** always looks like he knows where he is going
9) **Voice:** stern, authoritative with a slight New England accent
10) My guess for behavior strengths:

Main trend: **Builder**   Backup trend: **Planner**

Reasons: likes power, prestige, demands respect, takes charge of situations, leader, traditional, very dependable, is a strong driving force

11) Both card sort and Discover form confirms my observation

Jan is a **Builder** with a backup **Planner**. **Adventurer** qualities are not developed.

People Watcher's Form

- Name (Also give memory hook for remembering name if desired, e. g., Joyce Sharp - a person jumping for joy with a sharp knife):

- Age:

- Height:

- Weight:

- Head Shape:

- Hair:

- Forehead:

- Eyes:

- Nose:

- Ears:

- Hands:

- Clothes:

- Glasses and make-up:

- Body Language:

- Walk:

- Voice:

- My guess as to behavioral trend: Trend _____

- Backup _____

- Reasons:

If able to give card sort: 1st _____ 2nd _____ 3rd _____ 4th _____

As you read the descriptions of the *Planner,* **Builder,** Relater and Adventurer, keep these characters in mind because each of us is an individual and a unique mixture of all the colors.

Color Me a Unique Mixture

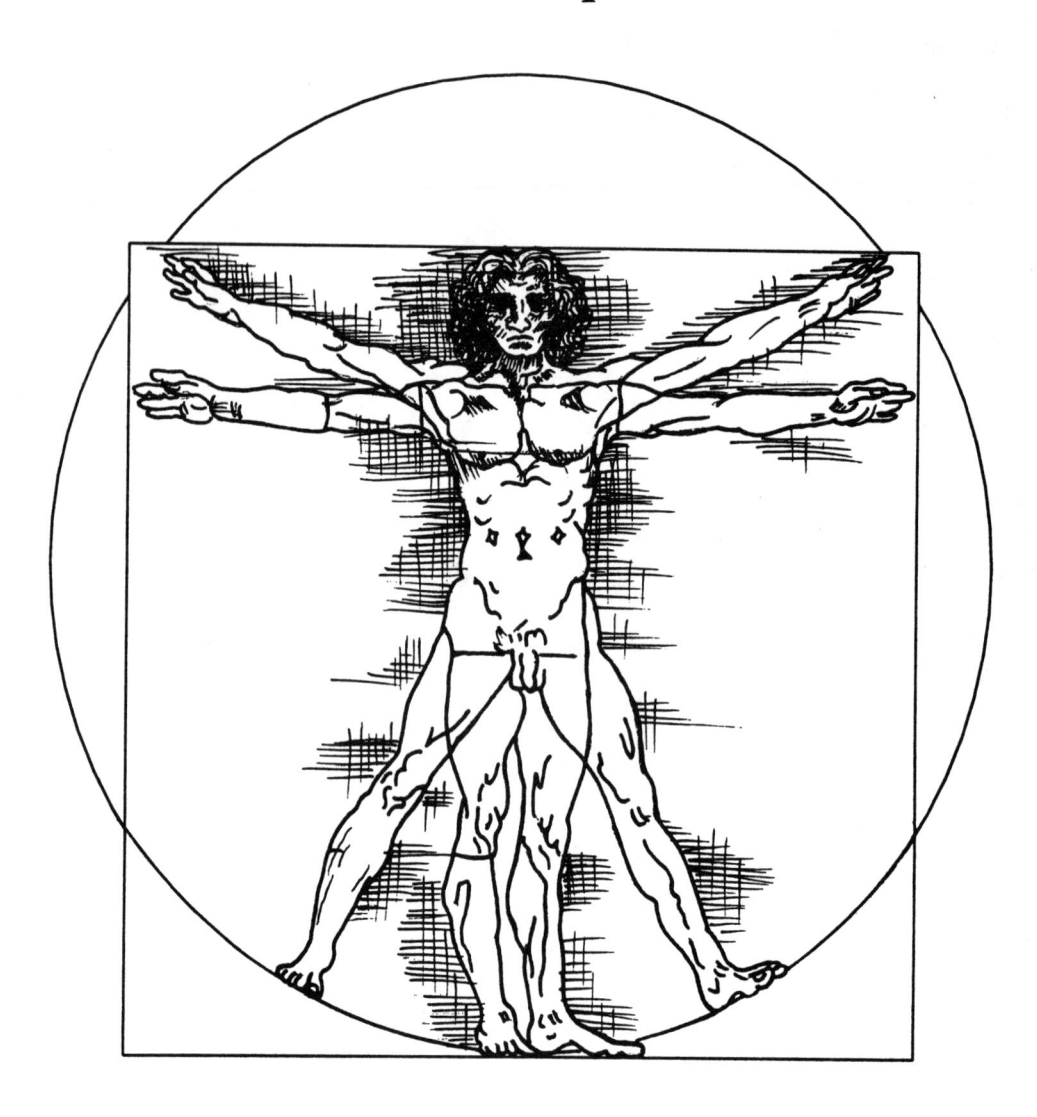

Step #5

The Four Parts of Self

A series of major behaviors are listed on the following pages.

A behavior is listed. Exercises for demonstrating or developing this behavior are given.

A strategy is suggested for dealing with anyone who demonstrates this behavior. Again, exercises for demonstrating or developing this behavior are given. If you already have this behavior, suggestions are given on how to use it to your advantage. More individual exercises for demonstrating or strengthening this behavior are given.

Finally, a model Personal Empowerment Assertion and a Career Connection are given in order to permanently develop these behaviors at a subconscious level. The purpose of these statements is to make these behaviors flow naturally when the occasion demands it, just as natural as blinking your eyes.

The behaviors are divided into the clusters indicative of the four parts of self:

Planner (thinking part of self),

Builder (deciding and leadership part of self),

Relater (feeling and team part of self),

Adventurer (action part of self).

How I Find Out About The *Planner* Part of Me

Some Observable Behaviors with Exercises for Developing Them

I may not have my act together but at least I know where all the parts are . . . .

Color My Behavioral Strength a Planner
Color Me Thinking

When the Planner part of self dominates, persons are prone to a lot of personal thinking. They want to cover all the details as a constant tumbling of ideas takes place in their minds. As a result, they generally ignore the external. They do not use their five exterior senses to the extent of the **Relater**.

However, their internal sense is perceptive, quick, and profound. This is the contradiction: they note interior rather than exterior detail. Sometimes this distraction may be of a more serious nature. **Planners** become so involved within themselves that they may have a serious mishap, e.g., while driving a car. This may lead to many accidents in their daily lives. On exams or job interviews, the need to cover all details rather than get to the bottom line may lose them precious marks in a **Builder** atmosphere where appreciation of the creative process is neither recognized nor rewarded. Usually it is necessary to give **Planners** more time.

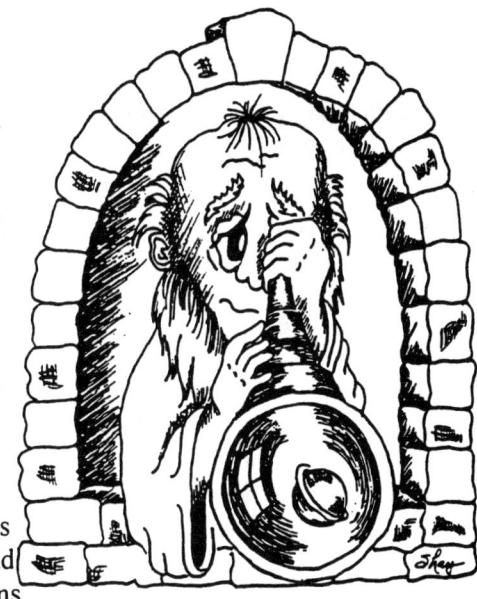

- If possible, watch Cirque du Soliel, it is a dramatic mix of circus arts and creative imagination flow. Further examples are the beginning of The Twilight Zone or the majority of the films of Steven Spielberg. The many ads and inserts on the SCI FI Channel are prime examples of right hemisphere thinking.

- Other examples of **Planners'** TV programs, films and books would include Stargate SGI, Children of a Lesser God, and Don Quixote. Can you think of examples of persons with strong right hemisphere thinking as indicated on the back of the **Planner** card? Write down several examples:

_____
_____
_____

Strategy for Developing/Working with Persons with this Behavior.

Remember that harsh anger at children for spilling milk because of distractions will only increase the **Planners'** withdrawal. Expect the same reaction from an employee. Realize that it takes **Planners** a longer time to accomplish a task or write an exam. It is not a matter of intelligence, but invested behaviors. "Patience" is the watchword in working with **Planners**.

Do You Have This Behavior? How to Use It to Your Advantage.

Practice and make it a daily challenge to remember exterior details, e.g., faces, names, clothing. Practice the People Watcher's List (p 27) daily. It would be a good idea to take questions that may be on an exam or on a job interview and bottom line the answers. Ask a **Builder,** who does well on such occasions, to give you examples.

- Check your **Planners'** responses to the People Watcher's list (p 27). Select a person to watch. Ask a **Relater** to watch the same person. Record your observations separately. Compare observations afterwards. Ask the **Relater** to point out exterior details that you may have missed.

My Career Connection: I will have a job that allows me time to do what I do best.

Your Personal Empowerment Statement: "Fantastic ideas pop up when I choose to relax and let my creative juices flow with no holds barred."

Color Me Creative... New And Better Ways

Bill Gates Catches the Boat

Planners' keen vision and thoughtful considerations enable them to see what is across the stream before others may. They are the discoverers of new and better ways. They are visionaries and a few like Bill Gates create a Microsoft empire or Walt Disney and the Disney empire.

Unfortunately, many others are not very practical. It often happens that, by the time they make up their minds to cross the river, others have taken their ideas and insights and run with them. They are people of missed opportunities. Usually they become quite upset when others have stolen their ideas. One of the authors experienced an acquaintance (**Planner**) who had developed an innovative, exciting motivational program. He had made an excellent living and gained national prominence. However, another acquaintance (**Builder**) sat through his program and copiously integrated his material into an action-packed seminar that he put into a video format within a decade. The **Builder** is a millionaire with hundreds of staff members making him a further fortune. The **Planner**, while living comfortably, is still a one-person business.

- Examine the lives of successful **Planners** like Bill Gates (Microsoft), David Ho (The Aaron Diamond Institute), Luc Montaignier (HIV research), Michelle Kwan and Kurt Browning (Olympic skaters), Jane Goodall Ph. D., (Anthropologist) Isabella Rossellini (international model), Walt Disney, Edison and Leonardo da Vinci in comparison to *The Pretender* or *Touched by an Angel.*

Strategy for Developing/Working with Persons with this Behavior.

Listen and put **Planners'** ideas into concrete, practical use. If you wait for them to implement their ideas, either you will be old and gray or others will have put their ideas to work.

- Education today faces many challenges: over-crowded classrooms, gang violence, lack of funding, lack of discipline, etc. Engage the creative right side of your brain. If you had the power to effect change, what idea would you institute? Write it down below.

_____
_____

- Make a dream list of all the things you would like to accomplish. Use your right-brain, possibility thinking. Do not let the left part of your brain criticize or negate. Write out your dream list. Turn your wishes into reality by making them a part of your 100 Lifetime Goals as discussed in Energizing The Internet of the Brain by Thoelke.

- **Planners'** see things other people miss. Review such art books as Arts and Ideas by William Fleming, Garden of Delights and the works of Hieronymus Bosch or the Paintings of Edward Hopper by Sherry Marker.

If You Have This Behavior, How to Use It to Your Advantage .

JUMP INTO THE WATER! THE ODDS ARE WITH YOU! LOOK INTO THE UNKNOWN!

- Refer to "How Thoughts Are Formed: Color Me Changing,....Succeeding."

My Career Connection: I will have a job that allows me to avoid distractions and does not limit my creativity.

Your Personal Empowerment Statement: I have a keen sense of accomplishment as I pause for a few moments each day and allow my mind to brainstorm possibilities. I act on my intuitions.

(Thoelke, Shay. <u>Energizing The Internet of the Brain</u>. Aeon Communications, Inc., Seattle WA 1997
Neilson, Stefan. *Color Me Changing Succeeding*   Aeon Hierophant, Seattle WA 1984

Color Me Searching Out The Causes

Dead Poets Society

Planners are not satisfied with any simple explanation, but wish to search out what makes them and others tick. They want to search out the causes. Consequently, they enter professions such as psychology and philosophy. No superficial explanation will satisfy. They want to know the "why" behind all the details. Their thoughts are long-ranged. They may spend their lifetimes dwelling on the future. Many times they are impractical heroes. They usually make excellent empathic listeners because of their need to know information in depth. The best chance of empathic ears may be found with **Planners**.

In the film Dead Poets Society, Robin Williams is a **Planner** with an **Adventurer** backup, who does battle with a total **Builder** establishment. The destructive results of only a **Builder** approach to every situation are aptly illustrated by the father of the youth who commits suicide and the expelling of Robin Williams from the academy. The last scene is a classic illustration of the revolution that takes place when people operate with all four parts of self. The youth that begins the revolution has powerful **Planner** behaviors. But he has been taught by Robin Williams to bring out the **Builder** part of himself when his personal convictions are violated. He stands up on the desk, in spite of the demand by the head of the academy, to sit down or be expelled. Others in the class follow his lead. The seeds of revolution have been planted.

- Watch films such as Dead Poets Society, Color Me Purple, The Hunt for Red October, Gorillas in the Mist, Children of a Lesser God to gain deeper insights about the **Planners'** value system.

- Review the new findings on Mars. Choose programs on the Discovery or TLC channel and you will see the **Planners'** investigative approach in action.

- Suggested readings of **Planner** characters in fiction would include: Of Mice and Men, Grapes of Wrath, Les Miserables, The Scarlet Letter, A Tale of Two Cities, Don Quixote de la Mancha, The Great American Bathroom Book (Page 5-D4-5)

Strategy for Developing/Working with Persons with this Behavior.

Constant silly talk bores them. They enjoy good humor, but if you approach them with trivia, you will have little chance of gaining their respect. Those with strong **Relater** behaviors must be especially aware of this. **Adventurers** who have an action bias should be aware that if they are constantly practical jokers or clownish, they've had it.

- <u>Tribute</u> is an excellent film that illustrates the difficult communication between a Relater/Adventurer comic father (Jack Lemon) and a serious **Planner** son (Bobby Benson).
- If you could be Bill Gates for 30 days, what would you do? Make a list of things. Remember a **Builder** will be seeking predominance and power. A **Relater** will want people situations while an **Adventurer** will be seeking travel and fun. As a **Planner** you would be seeking new systems.

_____
_____
_____
_____
_____

Do You Have This Behavior? How to Use It to Your Advantage.

You are often overly serious. Take a good course in learning how to laugh at life, especially at yourself.

- Examine the life of Charlie Brown as painted by Schultz.

- If you have a challenge, ask the question why? Keep asking this question until you find the source. For example: I have a headache. Why? Jim is always testing me. Why? I am shy. Why? I feel I'm dumb. Why? Keep asking "Why" until you discover the cause!

My Career Connection: I will have a job that allows me the freedom to investigate in-depth.

Your Personal Empowerment Statement: I take pride in asking questions and deciding for myself rather than the group. I have a sense of power in following what is right for me.

Color Me Cautious

The Caine Mutiny

It takes a considerable amount of time to gain the trust of people with strong **Planner** behaviors. They are very cautious and naturally suspicious. If you show an unfriendly manner, you will have difficulty gaining their confidence. You must prove over a period of time that you are worthy of trust. **Planners** will take considerable time in making decisions because they do not trust how their decisions will be received. Be prepared to have the patience of Job.

It is quite natural, if **Planners** see a group talking, for them to assume that the group is talking about them. If the group stops talking upon the arrival of the **Planner**, suspicions are confirmed. **Planners** seldom have the ability to allow the group the benefit of the doubt. The assumption that they are the subject of the group's conversation is almost automatic. Thus, their reactions to situations are extremely personal. For example, if you're late, the **Planner** concludes, "You don't want to be with me!" If you are crying or angry, "What did I do?"

- What are the signs of trust? There are three areas of trust to consider: physical, emotional and mental. A physical act of trust might be having someone serve as a spotter when you are pressing weights or making a move in gymnastics. It could be as simple as accepting a steadying hand when crossing over a log or climbing up a hill. An example of emotional trust is found in the film Dead Poet's Society when the students accepted a new style of learning from the instructor and allowed traditional values to be challenged. A pilot flying a plane must trust his instruments even if his mind wants him to believe he is flying upside down. This is an example of mental trust, instruments versus vertigo. List below three signs of trust based on your own experiences.

Physical trust?
_____
_____

Emotional trust?
_____
_____

Mental trust?
_____
_____

Strategy for Developing/Working with Persons with this Behavior.

Time is the main ingredient. If you are warm and kind, without going back on your word, you will win their confidence one step at a time. As **Relaters** are constantly changing moods, **Planners** have particular trouble being intimate with them.

How would you go about winning the confidence of a **Planner**?
_____
_____

Do You Have This Behavior? How to Use It to Your Advantage.

Always check out your suspicions. Give people the benefit of the doubt. Let them prove otherwise. Be mindful, the majority of people are more concerned about themselves and their own worlds than yours!

- Do you recognize this behavior in yourself? Record specific situations when this occurred and if you are comfortable share them with a friend.

_____
_____
_____
_____

My Career Connection: I will have a job that allows me to fit in and trust at my own pace.

Your Personal Empowerment Statement: I have a strong sense of power in making a decision and acting on the facts presently available. I am extremely flexible and change my actions as new information comes to me.

"You may have to fight a battle more than once to win it."

-Margaret Thatcher

Color Me Empathetic

Don't Cry for Me, Argentina

Even their own thoughts arouse their sympathy. They may easily begin to get excited or sad as they ponder over their own ideas. **Planners** have a continual, mysterious longing and searching for emotional and intellectual fulfillment. They have an aching of the heart. However, they do not show it on the outside. Because of these qualities, they are very understanding.

Although the exterior does not indicate it, like the outer warmth of the **Relater**, **Planners** are softhearted underneath. They know how to truly care. Because of their ability to be empathic, they are excellent listeners. Many times they form dependent relationships because of their willingness to listen to the troubles of the world. Possibly, because of their great difficulty in saying "No" to requests which commit them to difficult assignments such as committees or projects, they get themselves into difficult positions because they do not have the will power to quit, as the **Builder** does.

Although **Planners** are the carpenters of their own crosses, they will repeatedly complain that people are constantly taking advantage of them by burdening them with miseries. They have enough troubles of their own. That is probably true because they have vivid imaginations, which blow their difficulties completely out of proportion.

- Examine your own personal relationships. Do you play the role of dependent in any of them? Did you become involved in any relationships because of your inability to say, "No"? If you answered yes, begin asking yourself "Why?" until the final cause is found.

Strategy for Developing/Working with Persons with this Behavior.

- If you need an understanding ear to work out solutions you find too difficult to cope with yourself, your best chance for help is a **Planner**. Be aware of those who sympathize, rather than empathize. Sympathizing is stronger in the case of **Relaters**. Sympathetic **Planners** will listen intently and get so involved that they will not be able to be objective. If you decide to commit suicide, sympathetic **Planners** or **Relaters** may become so depressed with you that both of you jump out the window together. The authors have worked with many people involved in crisis telephone agencies. There is a shudder when sympathetic **Planners** and **Relaters** begin to tell us how they so charitably spent two or three hours listening to an alcoholic or drug addict over the phone. They probably increased the drug abuse by indulging the addict's tendency to self-pity. This arises from the **Planner's** inner need to know all the details and the **Relater's** need to talk. What is needed is "Tough Love"!

- Empathic **Planners** will be able to stand apart, as they usually have better control over their emotions. They will be warmly understood and helpful in aiding you in coming to the best solution for your difficulty. The accountability will be yours; if you decide to commit suicide, it will be your choice. An empathic **Planner** will be like a captain on a ship who throws out life preservers and all that is necessary to save you, but the ultimate choice will be whether you wish to accept help or not. As Colgrove, Bloomfield and McWilliams said in How to Survive the Loss of a Love:

> "THE QUESTION OF SUICIDE
> *Keep it a question*
> *It's not an answer.*"

- Make a list of people with whom you feel comfortable sharing confidences and why. These would be persons who you have found responsive when approaching on a personal level with your problems.

Person   Why?
_____   _____
_____   _____
_____   _____
_____   _____
_____   _____
_____   _____
_____   _____

Do You Have This Behavior? How to Use It to Your Advantage.

As you have a personal need to consider all the details, many may be interesting but unnecessary. Sometimes these details simply give rise to emotional confusion rather than clarity. You may lose friendship and power if you give in to this need to satisfy your curiosity.

- Make a list of decisions you may be avoiding and indicate why if you know the reason. You may have to do some honest self-digging.

_____
_____
_____
_____
_____
_____
_____

My Career Connection: I will use my empathic listening skills to further my career.

Your Personal Empowerment Statement: I listen to others in crisis when I choose and remain calm and in control of myself.

Color Me Planning

The World of the Computer

The computer is the brainchild of those with powerful **Planner** behaviors. The urge to understand, plan, predict, and explain reality dominates the **Planner's** life. All details and possibilities must be explored and mapped out before proper action may be taken.

Any ordinary performance is seen as falling short of what it should be. The whole pie, or *master plan,* must be examined with all its ingredients and interactions before the plan may be put into action. The computer is the extension of their minds.

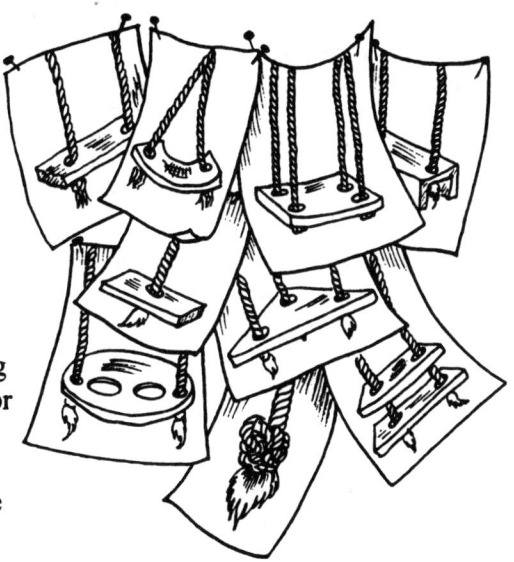

Using a creative **Planner** approach answer the following questions:

- What can be done to stop terrorism? How would you deal with Osama bin Laden, Islamic militant financier?

- How has the computer turned the world into a "Global Village?" What are the drawbacks to becoming totally linked to communication by the computer? What happens to personal privacy?

- What strategies would you suggest for making the Irish Peace Accord or the Palestinian/Israeli Peace Settlement successful?

- Consider the fears of a computer crash in the year 2,000. In your opinion, were these fears real or imagined? Why do you think it took so long to actively address the problem of Y2K?

- What strategies would you implement to contain Saddam Hussain or any other destructive leader who jeopardizes world peace?

- What are the advantages to using a **Planner** approach when tackling a difficult problem on the job or in one's personal life?

Strategy for Developing/Working with Persons with this Behavior.

Prepare for a long haul until perfection is attained (that is, if it ever comes.) You will probably have to put the plan into action before the **Planner** is satisfied or everything will always remain on the drawing board.

- If you are working with a **Planner** have he or she make a list of things that are on the drawing board. Upon completion of the list, prioritize it. Next develop a plan of action for item #1. Be sure the steps are concrete, reaching the goal of item # 1.

- If your primary strength is that of a **Planner**, complete the same process for yourself.

My drawing board list:

The prioritization of my drawing board list:

1. _____
2. _____
3. _____
4. _____
5. _____
6. _____
7. _____
8. _____
9. _____
10. _____
11. _____
12. _____
13. _____
14. _____
15. _____
16. _____
17. _____
18. _____
19. _____
20. _____

Goal of Item #1 and my plan of action. Use as many steps as necessary to achieve completion.

Goal _____

Plan of Action   **Date of Completion**

1. _____
2. _____
3. _____
4. _____
5. _____
6. _____
7. _____
8. _____
9. _____
10. _____

Do You Have This Behavior? How to Use It to Your Advantage.

It is better to light one candle than to curse the darkness. Allow the one candle to be lit. Do not put others to the *patience test*. Often, you act in slow motion. It may not seem slow to you so check out your actions with an **Adventurer** or **Builder**.

- We see the man in the moon. The strength of our investigative in-depth analysis and thought processes placed man on the moon.

My Career Connection: I will have a job that allows me to thoroughly plan before enacting.

Your Personal Empowerment Statements:
I conscientiously look at the pros and cons of three options, choose one and act accordingly.

> Three, two, one . . . "Roger" . . .
> They dared to reach for the stars
> Challenger's dream lives.
> ---Shay

Color Me Believing In Magic

Steven Spielberg and Disneyland

One of the greatest assets of **Planners** is a strong, creative, vivid imagination. It produces films such as Romeo and Juliet, Indiana Jones, Children of a Lesser God, E. T., The Lion King , Contact, Beauty and the Beast and all the magic of Disney films and Disneyland. This creativity has both its advantages and disadvantages. The world's greatest artists, poets, writers and scientists have a powerful **Planner part of self.** It is found in the music of Yanni, the voices of the Three Tenors, Domingo, Pavarotti and Carreras and the conducting of James Levine. However, with low self-esteem, this fertile imagination may create a world of monsters and demons that self-destruct as in the case of Van Gogh! The contemporaries of Van Gogh hung his paintings upside down in order to give public testimony as to their presumably poor artistic quality. Read Lust for Life by Irving Stone for a deeper understanding of Van Gogh. Nietzsche's philosophy dictated that the ultimate end of his philosophy was madness and being true to it, he went stark raving mad.

Planners possess the ability to imagine in-depth, to see the inner logical future conclusions or results of the present. Leonardo da Vinci's diagrams of the helicopter and tank, centuries before their invention, illustrate this visionary strength. The works of Jules Verne, Robert Heinlin, Isaac Asimov and other science-fiction writers are other such examples.

On the other hand, they may be given to brooding and daydreaming. They may truly live the Secret Life of Walter Mitty without any fruition or growth. Their imagination may also make mountains out of molehills. Combine this with their characteristic of suspicion, and an off-hand remark by you may be exaggerated into a personal attack.

Strategy for Developing/Working with Persons with this Behavior.

Be aware of the **Planners** tendency to exaggerate real and imagined offenses. Don't be fooled by the cool, calm exterior. Take advantage of their creative imaginations. They probably will be far ahead of their time.

- Watch the film Jumanji starring Robin Williams. It is a wonderful example of imagination exaggerated at its best.

- In working with **Planners,** it is important to check out the imagined hurts. Have them complete a list and check the validity of the items, e.g., check out a remark with a person: What do you mean by that?

- Do you dream? Have any of your dreams been exaggerations of real life situations?
  _____
  _____
  _____
  _____

- Have you ever analyzed your dreams? Could you go back and identify triggering events? Have you ever kept a dream log? Can you remember your dreams or is the next day just a blank? If this subject interests you check out a couple of books on dream analysis.

- Think back on a time when you were in a group and observed a painting. Did everyone see the same thing? How do different behavioral strengths have an impact on observational skills and interpretations?

_____
_____
_____
_____

If you want to see how behavioral strengths impact observational skills and interpretations check out a book containing the paintings of Edward Hopper. Select several paintings and ask a **Builder, Relater, Planner** and **Adventurer** what they see? The visions of the Shaman as seen through the imagination and creativity of the paintings of Susan Seddon would be another excellent resource.

Do You Have This Behavior? How to Use It to Your Advantage.

It is an absolute necessity for you to check out both real and imagined insults. Without personal insight, you may be embarrassed to discover the offenses are exaggerated fiction.

My Career Connection: I will have a job that allows my imagination to be used.

Your Personal Empowerment Statement: I enjoy writing poetry and allow my imagination to flow into my words.

Color Me Leading

The Ostrich

Planners make excellent leaders. However, there is a subtle contradiction in the inexperienced **Planners.** They want to lead, but the paradox is that they find it embarrassing to be the center of attention. Some may defer leadership to others even when they know they are the most qualified for the job. They will be angry that others were chosen before them. They may even become like Tam O'Shanter's wife in a poem by Robert Burns: "Nursing her wrath to keep it warm!" Shakespeare's Katherine in the Taming of the Shrew is another example. The willingness to take second place is not humility; it is the fear of disgrace. They also have a great deal of difficulty in correcting people on the spot. They will save up the mistakes of others until they explode. However, if they overcome this fear of public recognition, they will become powerful, creative, innovative leaders.

- It is important to use one's talents. When we hang back and do not use our talents or defer ourselves to standing in the shadows, we are not being accountable. Have you ever done this? If so list below the occasions when you have taken second place but knew you had the best idea and did not take the **ACTION STEPS** necessary:

  _____
  _____
  _____
  _____

- Listen to recordings of music with a **Planner** focus such as Mask in the Mirror (Celtic music with a Spanish influence), Puccini's Madame Butterfly, Pictures on Exhibition, Phantom of the Opera, and The Best of Enja by Loreena McKennitt.

Strategy for Developing/Working with Persons with this Behavior.

Basically, it is a matter of helping them overcome their fear of leading people. **Planners** need to learn to take accountability and responsibility for their actions. If they overcome their fears, the sky is the limit.

- If you are in a position to do so, put **Planners** in charge of a discussion group or in charge of a new responsibility on the job. Afterwards, ask them to share their feelings with you.

Do You Have This Behavior? How to Use It to Your Advantage.

Use your excellence! Learn to correct people at the time of the mistake, no brown stamp collecting (gunny bagging) for a later explosion! Start now! Secondly, it is okay to be less than perfect! It is okay to make a mistake! Above all, it is okay to admit it!

Think of a recent occasion when you regretted not confronting another's mistake or a situation. If you could go back in time, how would you deal differently with the situation? Explain in the space below:

_____
_____
_____

My **Career Connection:** I will have a job that lets me lead in my own way.

Your Personal Empowerment Statement: I take pride in being able to assume leadership when I know I am more capable than any other in the group.

Color Me Strong-Willed

"I have a dream" of Martin Luther King

Courageous and strong willed **Planners** have become the world's most powerful and creative leaders. Nothing, even the threat of death, hinders them from struggling toward the fulfillment of their convictions.

Some **Planners** need to work up their courage. They have a potentially strong will, but when their behaviors are undisciplined, they are prone to give up the ship in discouragement. One might picture the sinking of the Titanic. As the ship goes down, the **Builder's** arms will still be waving a flag above the water. Although a source of consolation, the undisciplined **Planners** would probably be the first to give up in despair and accept the fate of going down with the ship. **Relaters** would work toward everyone pulling together, maybe even in the wrong direction, but everyone would go down as a team! **Adventurers** might even instigate an ice floe party on the way down! Because of the **Planners'** needs to be competent and correct, they desperately fear the humiliation of failure. There is a contradiction for **Planners**. When **Planners** have made up their minds, come hell or high water, they will not be prevented from succeeding. On the other hand, if they have not made up their minds, they will go down with the ship accepting it as their fate.

- Think of a time when you gave up reaching a goal and might have succeeded if you had continued.

What was the goal and why did you withdraw your efforts?
_____
_____
_____
_____
_____
_____

- Now think of some challenges you overcame with dogged determination. What was the challenge(s) and how did you overcome it?
_____
_____
_____
_____
_____
_____

Strategy for Developing/Working with Persons with this Behavior.

Be aware of the **Planner's** possible discouragement. You will need to be a source of reinforcement and encouragement in difficult times.

- Identify the **Planners** in your personal life, circle of friends, classes or work. During the next week, look for occasions to give encouragement to these **Planners**. Journal your experiences below.

_____
_____
_____
_____
_____
_____
_____
_____
_____

Do You Have This Behavior? How to Use It to Your Advantage.

Misfortune is simply feedback to which you haven't taken the right approach!

Develop "Possibility Thinking!" It is better to have loved and lost than never to have loved at all. So too, it's better to have risked and lost than never to have risked at all. People, who avoid risk, fearing failure, may be missing many successes. It is taking risks that allows us to develop. Don't be someone who dies at 18 and is buried at 81. Risk-taking does not imply recklessness. It can be physical, intellectual or emotional. Mistakes are steppingstones to success. Learn from the **Adventurer!**

- When reading the following tombstone epitaph, one can only assume LES did not risk: *"Nothing Became His Life More Than the Leaving of it"* or *"Here lies LES MOORE; killed by 4 slugs from a 44; No LES, no MORE!"*
- Mistakes are stepping-stones to success. Misfortune is feedback to which one hasn't taken the right approach! Turn mistakes into learning situations and you will be creating steppingstones to success. Remember wallowing in mistakes is non-productive unless you have a thing for mud baths. Think of some misfortunes in your own life that have been learning experiences. List a few of them below and indicate how they served as personal steppingstones for you.

The Mistake:
_____
_____
_____

What I learned and how it became a steppingstone:
_____
_____
_____

The Mistake:
_____
_____
_____

What I learned and how it became a steppingstone:
_____
_____
_____

Career Connection: I will risk when it is necessary on the job.

Your Personal Empowerment Statement: I proceed with a dogged determination until I reach my goal. State the goal in concrete words.

A new idea is delicate. It can be killed with a sneer or a yawn; it can be stabbed to death by a quip and worried to death by a frown on the right man's brow.
-Charles Brower

Color Me Excited Inwardly

Mount St. Helens

The **Planner's** fierce emotional excitement is seldom allowed to surface. When it does, it may explode in a productive or distorted fashion. You might think of dormant volcanoes. Mount St. Helens was very peaceful and showed only a calm, cool exterior to the world. Then she blew her top. Even when she gave tips that she was ready to blow, those who lived in the peaceful valley below would not believe it possible that this quiet lady was capable of wreaking havoc. Harry Truman, an elderly resident of Spirit Lake below Mount St. Helens, paid dearly for his error.

Underneath their exteriors, **Planners** are like potentially seething caldrons. If you combine the emotional aspect with a vivid imagination, you will understand how they might conjure up monsters out of sheep. On the outside they will not show that they are affected by insults. Inside they will begin to boil as they mentally repeat those insults over and over. This, of course, will be until the explosion point. Many times the explosion is quite out of proportion to the indignity suffered. Consider the fears that may arise in the child while alone in a room at night! The movie Poltergeist is such an example.

Think of a post being driven into the ground. Negative comments, hurts and insults are like hammer blows that drive the post deeper and deeper into the ground. The deeper it is, the harder it will be to pull out. So it is with both real and imagined indignities suffered by the **Planners**. The indignities sink deeply and are extremely difficult to erase from the mind and the memory. Likewise, kindness and warm remarks are equally engraved in their minds

The **Builder, Relater** and **Adventurer** usually deal with their anger immediately and move on to other things. By contrast the **Planner** will store it up and not handle it immediately. Even after dealing with it, the **Planner** will push the replay button again and again analyzing whether the anger was handled correctly or could have been handled differently.

Be aware that the **Planner** hears the interior. There is the **Planner** in all of us. Think of a time when you thought you had clearly communicated an idea or emotion. It was not received in the manner in which you sent it. The receiver was listening to the undertones, seeing the shades of gray.

- Think of examples of violence that you have seen, read or experienced which involved the explosion of pent up emotions. On the lines below cite one of those examples:

_____
_____
_____
_____
_____

Many domestic murders and acts of violence are often explosions of stored emotions. Consider road rage. What are some ways a person could relieve this stored up energy, e.g., talking it out, writing it out, keeping a dream log? List your ideas below:

_____   _____
_____   _____
_____

Strategy for Developing/Working with Persons with this Behavior.

Don't believe that there is also a calm interior no matter how placid the **Planner** appears. Beneath it will be an abundance of either positive or negative emotion that has been suppressed. You might receive the outburst when you least expect it. *Positive emotion may be suppressed as well as negative.*

- Think of your experiences when you thought your comments were being well received. Suddenly there was an unexpected explosive response from the recipient of your remarks. Why did it happen and how did you feel?

_____
_____
_____
_____

Do You Have This Behavior? How to Use It to Your Advantage.

Learn how to allow your emotions to ventilate at the time of communication. Your constant holding onto hurts is non-productive and can be destructive. Your method of thinking over the insult is as if the insult were repeated once again in real life. Your mental replays of emotional experiences are as strong as reality. You will destroy both your creativity and relationships with people with negative imaginings. You are what you think!

- List some imagined and real insults you have experienced.

_____
_____
_____
_____

- Use the affirmation process to deal with imagined and real insults in a positive manner.
- List films you can think of where the role of the Planner is emphasized, e.g., <u>Stand by Me</u>, <u>Goodwill Hunting</u>, <u>The Prince of Tides</u>, <u>Lord of the Dance</u>

_____
_____
_____

My Career Connection: I will have a job that allows me to release my driving emotions.

Your Personal Empowerment Statement: I use that powerful excitement as a driving force in reaching my goal (state the goal in concrete fashion).

Color Me A Revolutionary

Princess Diana: A Stranger in a Strange Land

If they have not learned to control their behavior, **Planners** have a certain uneasiness in any group. Recall the difference in meeting the public between President Bill Clinton and Vice-President Al Gore. You will notice **Planners'** nervous body language when any spotlight shines, even dimly, on them. Consider Princess Diana in her early public exposure. It was only with intense coaching and training by Richard Attenborough that it became possible for her to appear "relaxed" outwardly when dealing with the public. **Planners** who have not developed **Builder** behaviors will turn all colors of the rainbow when asked to speak in front of others. At the same time, they can give magnificently clear soliloquies. **Planners** are natural-born hermits. They enjoy being alone and reviewing their own thoughts.

In a way they are *Strangers in a Strange Land*! They desperately want to fit in and be with people, yet feel uncomfortable with a group. There is a sort of yearning for a shelter, a better land or better conditions. The Psalms in the Old Testament are perfect examples of the **Planners'** way of thinking. They are forever searching for faraway green pastures. **Planners** many times are oblivious to the grass immediately under their feet. They would like to be the charismatic leader. Yet, they are uncomfortable standing in front of the masses and leading.

No interior detail escapes their keen observation. But, they may make poor use of their exterior senses, especially in contrast to the **Relater.** They are very often distracted when in groups and in their own environment. They may miss many exterior details.

- Most Science Fiction is the creation of **Planners** such as Heinlein's *Stranger in a Strange Land*. Jung (psychologist) noted that the world is a series of opposites. He indicated that each person has an unconscious shadow or opposite to one's conscious life indicated in dreams. What ingredients contribute to the positive use of the imagination - see, feel and express? List several on the lines below:
  _____
  _____

Strategy for Developing/Working with Persons with this Behavior

Be patient and understand the motivation of those with strong **Planner** behaviors. In most cases, it will be well worthwhile, for you will find a fountain of creativity.

- Write three Personal Empowerment Statements around increasing patience, understanding and perseverance. They will serve you well when dealing with the **Planners** in your life.
1. _____
2. _____
3. _____

Do You Have This Behavior? How to Use It to Your Advantage.

Take a course in positive image development. See, feel, and experience yourself giving a speech in a cool, clear, calm manner.

- Read such books as <u>I'm O K, You're O K</u>. <u>The Road Less Traveled</u> by M. Scott Peck is also an excellent resource.

My Career Connection: I will have a job that is open to innovation.

Your Personal Empowerment Statement: I am calm, cool, collected and dynamically persuasive when I speak in public at (name the occasion remembering to see it and feel it).

Color Me A Genius

Uddlemay Asesphray

One of the quickest ways to identify **Planners** is to listen to their jumbled up, muddled phrases. They usually leave sentences unfinished and stutter over words. This is particularly true when the situation is important. You will need to be a broad jumper many times when you are speaking with them. They will skip from idea to idea, expecting you to fill in on several thoughts that they have already processed, but not shared along the way. This happens especially when they are excited about their subject. The reason is that **Planners** are creative and ideas come so rapidly, their mouths can not handle them quickly enough.

- If **Planners** are a part of any cooperative group or team presentations in your life, offer them opportunities to give short talks. Help them prepare very simple bottom line presentations.

- If you are a group leader, pair off either a **Builder** or an **Adventurer** with a **Planner** in preparing a presentation to the group. If you are a manager at work, team your **Planner** employees with other color strengths. Plan your shifts carefully and you will create winning teams.

Strategy for Developing/Working with Persons with this Behavior.

If you join in on the excitement of the ideas and they are creative, you will obtain a considerable amount of information. Develop your empathic listening skills and this will help you understand all the subtleties. **Relaters, Builders**, and **Adventurers** often miss the profundity of the **Planners'** conversation.

- Practice your listening skills in time slots of four or five minutes with a **Planner.**

- Encourage the **Planners** in your life to take speech, oral interpretation or debate classes. Suggest to **Planners** they obtain speaker information from a Toastmaster's club, joining one if possible. Set up such a club in the school. Obtain information from the National Speakers' Association.

Do You Have This Behavior? How to Use It to Your Advantage.

A very brilliant and creative **Planner** used the following example to explain his creativity. Imagine being in a large stadium in the evening with all the lights turned on brightly. Now, bring all those lights into a single room. Everyone would be blinded. The **Planner** genius must learn to let only one light shine at a time if he/she is to survive!

Public speaking courses where you may proceed at your own pace are a must. Join a drama group and tryout for roles. Volunteer for understudy parts. Even if you never play the role, you will have the experience of practicing the role. Such training is critical if you desire to be a success in the educational, business or social world. Practice giving out your ideas in a slow, concise, logical sequence. Use audio and video recorders so that you may both hear and see yourself in action. Above all learn that you do not throw pearls to swine!

- Draw up a list of local places where you may develop your speaking skills, e.g., school councils, community service organizations, neighborhood councils, school board, PTA meetings, a local drama group, a book club, toastmasters.

My Career Connection: I will want a job that allows me to be assertive and confident.

Your Personal Empowerment Statement: I am a rock in a stream. All the negative put-downs flow past me like rushing water. I am a solid strong rock. I am a rock.*

* <u>Energizing, The Internet of the Brain</u> by Shay Thoelke, Aeon Communications, Inc., 1998

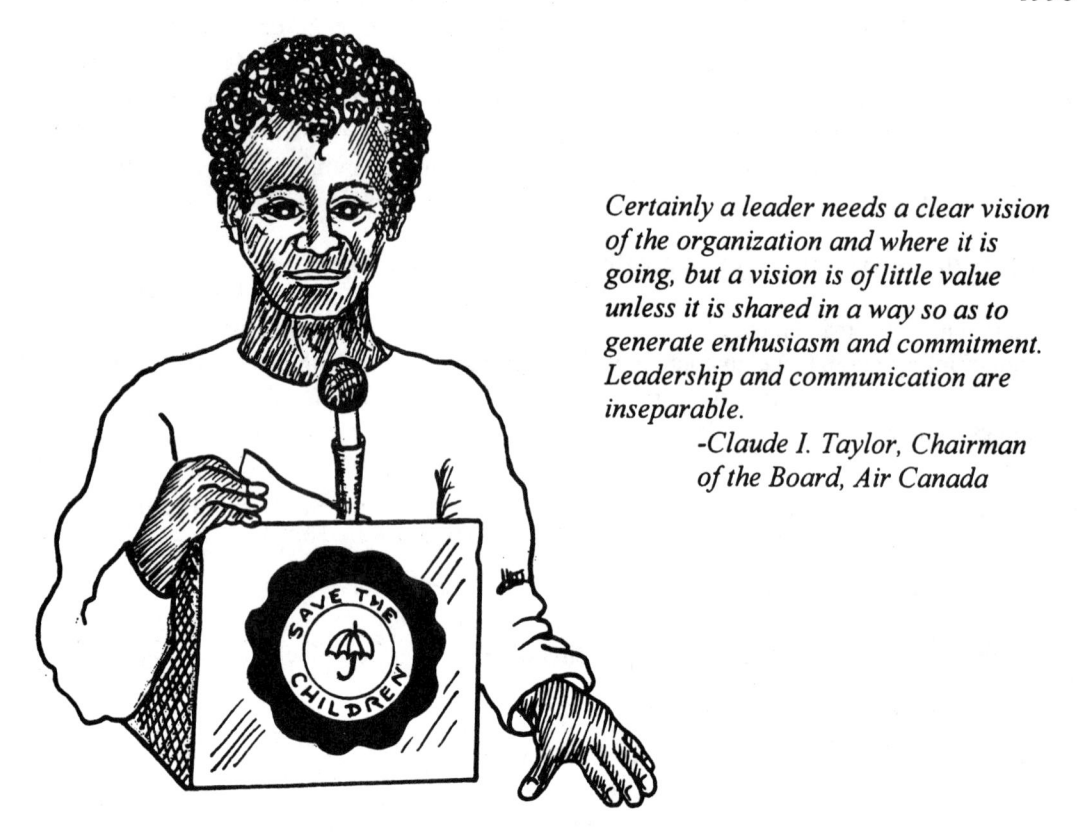

Certainly a leader needs a clear vision of the organization and where it is going, but a vision is of little value unless it is shared in a way so as to generate enthusiasm and commitment. Leadership and communication are inseparable.
  -Claude I. Taylor, Chairman of the Board, Air Canada

Color Me Compassionate

The Struggle

Planners' compassion, empathy, and caring rises from their own pain and understanding of the challenge to communicate in depth with their fellow humans. A Greek legend speaks of how humankind was, at a time, one. However, man rebelled and the gods split humankind in half. Since that time man has always been in search of his other half.

Planners seldom speak among strangers. When they do speak, it is usually only with those they trust. Consequently, many may think that they are cold, aloof and withdrawn. In the majority of cases, this is not true. They have not acquired the exterior communication skills that the **Relaters/Builders/Adventurers** possess. Therefore, although there is a deep inner desire to form friendships and communicate, there is a difficulty in forming new relationships. The uneasiness that you may sense in their presence is actually their uneasiness in introducing themselves.

As illustrated by Kirlian photography, we know an aura, an energy field, is given off by the human body. You may sometimes sense this aura. In today's language we often refer to this as receiving someone's vibrations. Most often this occurs with **Planners** and in turn they are the most sensitive receivers. While **Planners** may emit a strong aura, words do not come easily for them.

Unfortunately, even when **Planners** are brave enough to take the initiative to introduce themselves, their words come out in a rather muddled-up fashion. It takes a great deal of inner exertion for them to manifest themselves. Thus, even after an introduction you may still feel the waves of uncomfortable uneasiness. **Planners** desperately want to describe their inner life to others, but cannot; the **Relaters** do this comparatively easily; **Adventurers** would find this self-analysis boring and **Builders** can do so, but do not want to be put at a disadvantage.

Strategy for Developing/Working with Persons with this Behavior.

As mentioned, if you have the opportunity to have input into a **Planner's** education and development, encourage participation in public speaking.

- Approach **Planners** in a warm and friendly manner. At the same time, do not crowd their physical space.

- If you are the leader in a discussion group, provide **Planners** with a safe framework. Do not call on them first. Allow them time to sort and tumble their ideas. You will sense when they feel comfortable enough to share.

Do You Have This Behavior? How to Use It to Your Advantage.

Practice introducing yourself first and make the initial movement of friendliness.
- Challenge yourself to initiate an introduction to a stranger each day for a week.

My Career Connection: I will make an effort to fit into the group on the job.

Your Personal Empowerment Statement: I have a deep sense of compassion for my fellow human being (name the person) who is struggling with (name the situation.)

Call Me Persevering

The Hare and the Tortoise

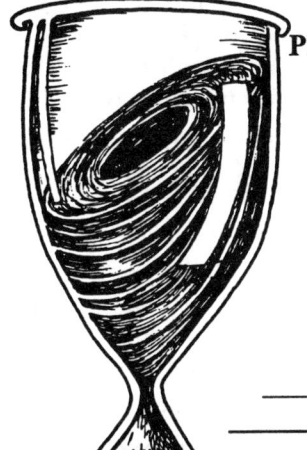

Planners' patience and perseverance are without equal. It is said that Edison made at least ten thousand experiments before perfecting the light bulb. His philosophy was that there was no such thing as failure, only steppingstones to success. Each so-called "failure" brought him one step closer to his goal. Give the **Planners** time and space and their creativity will blossom forth in glory.

- Haste makes waste. What are the advantages of having or not having a plan?

_____
_____
_____
_____

Strategy for Developing/Working with Persons with this Behavior. Make sure you give **Planners** time and a quiet place where they can think. Their ideas are usually well thought out. They will continue with their ideas until proven wrong. Don't expect an immediate response. Putting **Planners** on the hot seat is doomed to failure.

- Consider the atmosphere that surrounds interviews and job testing. Which personality style would be able to handle the pressures of these encounters best? Why?

_____
_____

Do You Have This Behavior? How to Use It to Your Advantage.

Recognize that you may take longer to reach decisions and perform tasks. Incorporate adequate time into your daily schedule.

- How might you, as a **Planner**, position yourself for controlling limited situations? What could you do or what aids could you use so you would perform with greater ease?

_____
_____

My Career Connection: I will hold a job that values comprehensive planning.

Your Personal Empowerment Statement: I am patient and proceed with thrilling excitement in expectancy of reaching my goal (state the goal in concrete language).

The Adult Planner in Summary

Atlas gave a sigh of relief when you were born. Another person to help him in carrying the weight of the world on his shoulders. From the very beginning, you were not thrilled with the idea of strangers picking you up or fussing over you. Your earliest career experiences involved investigation and research. What was the function of a wall plug? What things could be inserted? New toys were to be closely examined before accepting them. All dolls or action figures required modification. You cut off their hair, trimmed their eyebrows and exchanged their arms and legs. For many of you, your blanket represented security. Everywhere you went, it went. Some of you like Linus in Charlie Brown, still have it or at least a portion of it. Seasonings in spice bottles were boring. They looked much better after you had layered and mixed them. Dr. Seuss was fine, but repetition became boring to you. Winnie the Pooh and Fairy tales with surprise endings were more fascinating. You tried the role of engineer as you tested Archimedes' principles in the toilet bowl. Potatoes and thread spools floated. Watches sank. At a young age you considered psychiatry or counseling. Your parents' insistence on the idea there was only one Santa concerned you. Anyone who was halfway observant knew there were multiple Santas. You could find them in malls, opening doors and ringing bells by little red buckets on every street corner. Sometimes your vivid imagination caused you grief as monsters took up residency in your closet and under your bed. You trained as a gymnast until you could go from your door to your bed without touching the floor. Stray dogs and cats knew they would find a home with you. All they had to do was look lost and the humanitarian in you felt an obligation to take care of them. Some of them fell apart. You thought it was great. One cat multiplied into mommy and five kittens.

The first day of school was a frightening experience. You were certain your parents were abandoning you to a great yellow container. By your standards, your classroom was noisy and chaotic. Because you wanted to be prepared, you of course had a box of 64 Crayolas. All of the **Adventurers** wanted to borrow your crayons and returned them to your box out of order, blunted and with the wrappers half torn off. The **Adventurers** were teaching you a lesson. What was theirs was theirs and what was yours was theirs. If the **Relaters** borrowed your crayons, they promptly shared them with other **Relaters**. And you instinctively knew it would not be wise to ask the **Builders** if you could borrow a missing color.

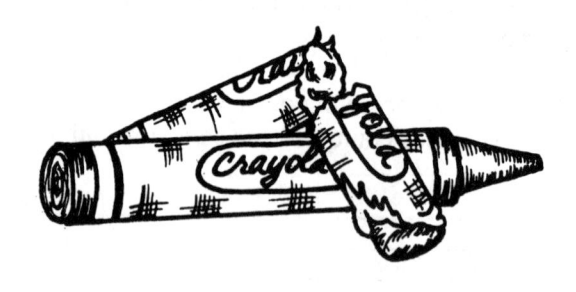

You enjoyed show and tell as long as your classmates were doing the sharing. You didn't enjoy being the sharer for fear of ridicule. Timed tests would almost prove your undoing. Three minutes did not allow you to check the accuracy of your answers and to put them down in a neat and orderly manner. You knew you were intelligent and couldn't understand how a clock was a fair evaluation of your abilities. You were already analyzing.

The beginning of middle school was a painful process. Everyone but you seemed to know the rules of survival: Push, shove, laugh, tell jokes, copy each other's work, tease the girls and flirt with the boys. You did know with total certainty that the inventor of underarm deodorant should have been awarded the Nobel Peace Prize. There were moments when you were certain puberty would never pass. Zits blossomed like the oil fires of Kuwait. Your first dance was comparable to attending a hanging. High school approached and you heard rumors of freshman being permanently entombed in lockers. The thought of joining a convent or monastery began to sound appealing.

Finally, high school. Sure enough lockers were involved. The locker partner from hell was assigned to you. Your only defense was to carry all your books, making you appear as a total nerd. You tried to blend into the woodwork. No such luck! Another life lesson to be learned. Sometimes you did get lucky and instead of being the focus of a joke you got to listen. Confidently you took your place in the circle. You knew you were a good listener. Even though you were a good listener, jokes were an enigma to you. You could hear a joke more than once, but because you concentrated on the nuances of telling it, the punch line was often lost on you. Any attempts on your part to retell a joke usually ended with you messing up the punch line. Even today punch lines often continue to elude you until you have replayed the joke several times. The saying, "He who laughs last, laughs best." must have been referring to Planners. At the same time your wit can be razor sharp if the thought originates with you and you feel comfortable sharing.

If you walked up to a group and they stopped talking, you assumed they had been talking about you. The lunchroom for you was a study in people. While the **Relaters** were checking out the appearances of everyone, you were monitoring for inner detail by scanning the surrounding conversations. As a youth you did not rush into relationships and friendships. As an adult, you still test the waters of relationships and friendships carefully. Your trust has to be earned, but once you commit you are in for the long haul. Criticism directed at you can be devastating if you internalize it. You will replay the criticism until it is ground into your psyche. You would take issue with the person who said "Sticks and stones will break your bones, but words will never hurt you." It is a quality **Builders, Adventurers** and **Relaters** do not understand. Either view criticism as means to self-growth or let it flow downstream.

Failure for you is personal. You collect guilt like barnacles on a pier. Get out the scraper. It is a rejuvenating process.

When confronted with a project, you feel obligated to thoroughly research the topic. Throwing something against the wall is not your style. To you, such an approach, lacks integrity. Developing and deciding on a focus for you is a challenge. You view a singular focus as limiting. Once you begin the actual project, your <u>thoroughness</u> will usually produce too much volume because of your <u>need to explain everything in-depth and detail</u>. If you want an example of detail in-depth, go to the library and check out a copy of a translation of one of DaVinci's original notebooks. Look up a topic like light or water. His writing is as detailed as his sketches. Like DaVinci, conciseness does not come easily to you. Editing and cutting is always an agonizing process.

Deadlines are burdensome. Your thoroughness and penchant for detail are assets You always want more time for refining the final product. When this happens, remember Leonardo. He had the same problem with his paintings. Consequently, because he continually sought perfection, he only completed 13 paintings in his over eighty years of life. Your **Planner** strengths will serve you well in the fields of astronomy/scientific scholar (Carl Sagan), publishing and dentistry.

It is suggested **Planners** cannot meet deadlines or make bottom-line decisions. Consider the **Builder's** decision making process: What is the situation/the problem today? Based on the information I have, what I presently know today, I will make the decision. If circumstances change in five minutes or five days, I will adjust and make another decision. In the same situation the Planner finds such a response unacceptable. Your tendency is to think, "I have all this information today, but I want to wait for the next minute because new information, possibly crucial information, might come in that would impact my decision." Learn from the **Builder**. There are times when a score of 94 to 99% is acceptable. Pick and choose those battles that require 100%. If you are a neurosurgeon performing surgery then yes, 100% is required. If you are landscaping an arboretum and are short ten plants for the Japanese reflection pool, spread out the existing plants. Be realistic in your quality assessments. Take control of your time and effort rather than being controlled by them.

<u>When you begin a project or become a part of a cause it can become all consuming</u>. Undertake a research project and your desk will disappear beneath a pile of papers. While the stacks will drive you crazy, you know where every resource, every notation written

on a scrap of paper, is located. Your production style is disconcerting to the **Builders** and **Relaters**. Begin a painting and you need to complete it whether it is a canvas or the ceiling of the Sistine Chapel.

Start a novel or a non-fiction book and you will read it from start to finish. You are not comfortable starting multiple books. Like a rotation eater who eats one course at a time, you don't want the plot or content muddied. By contrast, the Relater and the Builder can be reading several books at a time. When a book doesn't captivate you or is poorly written, it is a struggle for you to set it aside. You feel obligated to finish anything you begin. You are the editor every author is seeking.

<u>If you feel passionately about a cause, you will spend a lifetime achieving it</u>. Mandela, Edelman and Jacques Cousteau are such examples.

As passionate as you may be about a cause, you may have to temper your approach to achieve your goal. A presentation to **Relaters**, **Builders** or **Adventurers** will have to be customized if you are seeking their support. Consider the case of Jocelyn Elders, the controversial former U.S. Surgeon General. She passionately believes the education system must "teach that fourth R: responsibility. Our bright young people are out in an ocean surrounded by the sharks of drugs, alcohol, guns, suicide. And we are sitting on the beach, sipping from our fountains of 'Just Say No.' " She further believes health education should be taught in the schools, "from kindergarten through 12th grade, including everything from proper nutrition to sex education." The response to her position was to attack her for "wanting to teach children about sex." She was forced to resign because of her views. Political agendas were also a factor. Projects involving advocacy, reform, political action and the environment will serve your **Planner** needs. Success will depend upon your ability to speak all four languages.

<u>The humanitarian within you is deeply seeded</u>. <u>You are compassionate and have a reverence for life</u>. You want to improve the quality of life

Because I have confidence in the power of truth, and of the spirit, I have confidence in the future of mankind.
      ---Albert Schweitzer

You find acceptable the concept of Justice being blind while she renders fair judgment. It is unacceptable to be blind to injustice. Your assets include tenaciousness and a capacity for patience. You will stick to a project until its completion. In research you will dig your way to China to achieve your objective. Combine your tenacity and patience with humanitarian motivation and you are a formidable force.

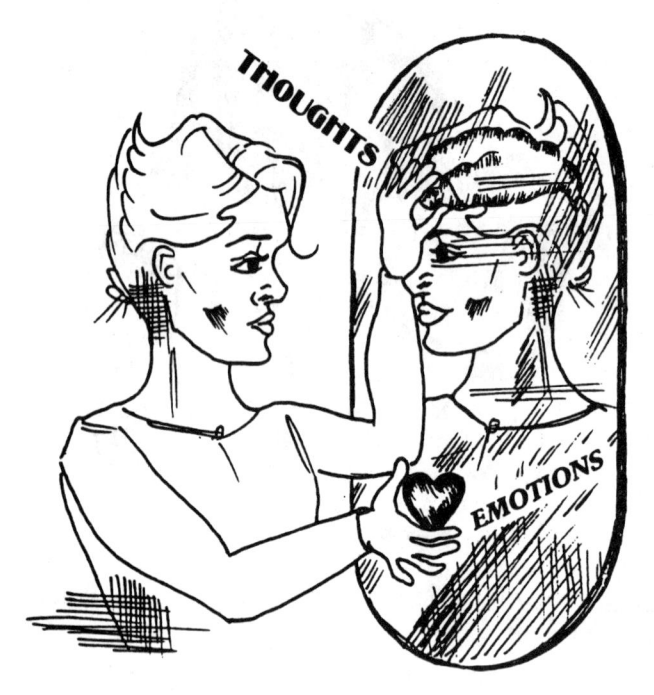

Your motivation of internal analyzing goes hand in hand with planning, designing, budgeting, innovation and logical thought. You are motivated to explore the unknown. View the architectural works of Louis Sullivan (The Wainwright Building), Frank Lloyd Wright ("Falling Water" House and the Guggenheim Museum), Le Corbusier (Notre-Dame-du-Haut), Eero Saarinen (Trans World Flight Center, Kennedy International Airport), I.M. Pei (National Gallery and the Glass Pyramid of the Louvre) and you will see this motivation in action.

When the **Planner** sets aside the known, the unknown becomes a reality. Needing a vehicle for transportation on the moon, you set aside all you knew about 4-wheel conveyances and created the moonwalker. Wanting an elevator into space, you developed the space shuttle. The computer of yesterday filled a room. A young man at 18 in partnership with Paul Allen, recognizing that personal computers would ultimately become widespread in their use, formed Microsoft. Today Bill Gates is chairman and CEO of Microsoft Corporation, the leading provider of computer software worldwide. Now that room sized computer fits in your hand and tomorrow . . .?

You are a visionary and a futurist. Add to these two qualities your ability to imagine in-depth and you become R. Buckminster Fuller. We remember him as the father of the geodesic dome, but he was so much more. The following quote by Buckminster Fuller explains his motivation: "You belong to the universe. Your significance will remain forever obscure to you, but . . . you are fulfilling your role if you apply yourself to converting your experience to the highest advantage of others." Like author and futurist Alvin Toffler said, "We must choose to control our technology rather than being controlled by it." He did it. He was an architect, engineer, mathematician, cosmologist, inventor and true visionary. Felissimo in awarding him the Tribute 21 said, "His primary goal was to anticipate and solve humanity's major problems through the highest technology by providing us with more support using less resources. His accomplishments toward that goal were many and wide-ranging. His designs, his research into renewable resources, and <u>innovative methods</u> for <u>problem-solving</u> will continue to <u>benefit humanity</u> for many years to come." Review the descriptive terms underlined in this paragraph and you have the M.O. (Motivational Operandi) of a Planner.

The Planner <u>vision, commitment to the growth and development of humanity</u> is exemplified in the career of John Templeton. Examine the focus of his foundation: science and religion, spirituality and health, character development, free enterprise and grant opportunities. "Recognizing the importance of character and virtue in a free society, the John Templeton Foundation supports a broad spectrum of programs including publications and studies that promote the importance of character education during childhood, adolescence and young adulthood . . . In 1987, Sir John Templeton initiated the *Laws of Life Essay Contest* in his hometown of Winchester, Tennessee. His <u>vision</u> was to encourage young people to write about their own 'laws of life.' Contests now take place in communities and schools throughout the United States and in many other countries . . . During the 1997-1998 school year, over 45,000 young people wrote a Laws of Life Essay."
(Quoted from the John Templeton Foundation, http://www.templeton.org/sirjohnbioasp).

Investor Peter Lynch used his strength as a researcher while managing Fidelity's Magellan Fund from 1977-1990. During his thirteen years of management, Magellan became the top-ranked equity mutual fund in the country. An investment of $1,000 in Magellan in 1977, when Lynch started, was worth $28,000 in 1990 when he stepped down. How did he achieve such success? Peter Lynch explains he is a bottom-up type of investor. First he finds companies that he feels have "good stories." After he identifies these companies, his next step is to do <u>in-depth research</u> to see if the company is a good investment. This differs from a top-down approach where the first step is an overall economic forecast and narrowing the focus down to sectors, industries and finally companies expected to perform well. He continues to put into practice the process of exploring all the options which in turn leads to exploring new options.

> *Oh, the comfort, the inexpressible comfort of feeling safe with a person; having neither to weigh thoughts nor measure words, but to pour them out, just as they are, chaff and grain together, knowing that a faithful hand will take and sift them, keep what is worth keeping, and then, with the breath of kindness, blow the rest away.*
> *—George Eliot*

As a **Planner** educator you will be concerned about imparting information with integrity. You will encourage the exploration of ideas and freedom of thought because this approach is a motivational force within you. You are open and sensitive to the learning styles of others. You will not lock in on a single delivery system. You will encourage others to investigate and to risk intellectually. While some may mistake your exterior actions as focusing on content, the opposite is true. <u>You are concerned with interior detail</u>. When someone talks to you, you hear the intonations and you hear what is not being said. This quality will also serve you well especially if you are in the field of consulting, counseling, psychology, psychiatry or medicine.

Some people may think you are cool and aloof because you tend to be reticent. You need to survey the lay of the land before you "move out." When a **Relater** enters a room there is a sense of vibrancy. The room's energy level goes up when an **Adventurer** arrives on the scene. The **Builder** brings an aura of confidence when entering. Your vibrancy, your energy lies just beneath a calm appearance. You will release it on your terms. It is a quality emulated by models, negotiators, mediators and counselors.

There is a contradiction in your desire to be in front, but not comfortable in the spotlight. Any performing art offers you the opportunity to wear a mask and step into the spotlight. Your strength of seeing interior detail will provide you with insight of any character you play. As you develop your **Builder, Relater** and **Adventurer** strengths, the process will become easier for you.

<u>You are content to work independently</u>. Working at home is a viable choice for you. You enjoy working in an environment free of distractions. This does not mean you are an isolationist. You will always call upon others for their input if it will enhance what you are doing or creating. The computer is a wonderful outlet for you. It allows you privacy in the creative process. At the same time it affords you unlimited access to the information highway.

The creative drive for you differs from the other colors. <u>Your motivation to explore the unknown, the never before, sets you apart as an artist. You are visionary</u>. You see what is not there. Before you were twenty-five you created what is considered to be the greatest sculpture in the world, the Pieta. Most of us, if confronted with "The Giant," a flawed block of marble, would have seen just a block of marble. As Michaelangelo, you saw *David* waiting to be released. At the entrance to the Dachau Memorial you saw skeletal figures in the form of barbed wire when you created the sculpture. As Frederick Hart on the front tympanum of the Washington National Cathedral, your vision of "Ex Nihilo" (Out of Nothing) swirled and flowed out of stone. With a tripod, backpack and camera as Ansel Adams you opened up a world of beauty for us through your black and white photography. Today as Bev Doolittle you challenge us to find the hidden content in your "camouflage" paintings. Your boulders become buffalo, your bushes contain the watchful faces of Indians, rocks and snow become a herd of pinto horses. Doolittle, explaining her art, said, "Many people call me a 'camouflage artist,' but that doesn't really fit. If I have to categorize at all, I prefer to think of myself as a 'concept painter.' I am an artist who uses camouflage to get my story across, to slow the viewing process so you can discover it for yourself . . ." Elise Maclay, a writer and poet in her own right, describes the **Planner** creativity of Doolittle in <u>BEV DOOLITTLE New Magic</u>.

"Bev Doolittle is one of the most astonishing artists of our time. Her unique vision and talent combine to create images that evoke a desire to enter her world, to look beyond what the viewer immediately sees. It is, in fact almost impossible to view a Doolittle painting passively. One is drawn in-to speculate, to wonder, to explore the Power of myth and meaning behind the brilliant execution and beauty of the painting itself."

With your focus on the thorough examination of possibilities, you are often considered too serious by other personalities. When this happens, know you are invaluable to the successful completion of any project. You are willing to invest whatever time and effort is necessary to cover all the options, before making a decision or reaching a goal. When you are exploring the unknown, there will be those who call you a dreamer. 2

All men dream; but not equally. Those who dream by night in the dusty recesses of their mind wake in the day to find it was vanity;
but dreamers of the day are dangerous men, for they may
act their dreams with open eyes, to make it possible.
T.S. Elliot, Seven Pillars of Wisdom

Nurture your ability to dream.

Your Communication Key (think):

Build an atmosphere of freedom of thought

Your secret vocabulary for:

- developing **Planner** behaviors

- getting along with people with strong **PLANNER** behaviors:

  - think * understand * discover * perfect * correct * listen * plan * new ways *
    * predict * inner life * change * mystery * cause *
    * invent * exactness * improve * science fiction * analyze *

PLANNER - GREEN

Comfort zone: Open to new and creative ideas; abstract thinking; the latest and most innovative procedures and product; prefers creative subject input that challenges the mind; quiet time, abhors triviality; not too concerned about dress, hair style or exterior details; future oriented (visionary) science fiction and exploration of space; revolutionary

Demands on people: Creative thinking; work alone; develop the mind and reasoning process to be logical - long and detailed explanations, reports and meetings.

**How to build powerful teams, self-esteem, success,
maximum productivity in others and reinforce leadership.**

* HOT BUTTONS *

When the **Planner (green) part of self** in a person is very strong,
consider what motivates that person and apply it.

- Take a serious approach to **Planners'** communications.
- Take a thoughtful, calm, cool and collected interest. Don't dominate with your ideas.
- Practice patience, allow and encourage personal creativity.
- Design work that provides more time for development and production than that of the **Builder**.
- Note time constraints limit **Planners'** productivity and do not indicate their capacity to be of service. Encourage **Planners** to take action and not use all their time in planning only.
- Give ample warning before calling on them to speak in public.
- When asking for comments at meetings, do not call on **Planners** first. They need more time to consider their responses.
- Giving harsh bottom line treatment causes withdrawal/feelings of inadequacy and incompetent work.

How I Find Out About The Builder Part of Me

Some Observable Behaviors with Exercises for Developing Them

Pawn or Checkmate?

Color Me In Charge

Color Me a Builder

Builders are practical people. They have built nations, empires, world religions and continue to do so. Men like John Adams and Thomas Jefferson laid the building blocks of America in the form of the constitution. Caesar created the empire of Rome and built entire road systems linking the west and east. All roads led to Rome. The Egyptians founded dynasties and built pyramids, which still stand today as one of the wonders of the world. **Builders** believe that they alone have the capacity to carry the world on their shoulders similar to Atlas. They are builders of homes, schools, businesses, corporations and multi-nationals. Whenever you see the Golden Arches, you know you are looking at the home of McDonald's where billions of hamburgers have been sold worldwide. **Builders** have the ability to channel their energy in one direction until success is achieved. In the field of publishing, Tina Brown, Editor of <u>Vanity Fair</u> magazine and recipient of "Editor of the Year" and Helen Gurley Brown, Editor of <u>Cosmopolitan</u> are excellent examples. Politically, Former secretary of State Madeline Albright, President Johnson, President Reagan and President George Bush stand side-by-side in their **Builder** strengths. In the field of broadcasting, we have watched such persons as Dan Rather, Diane Sawyer, Mike Wallace and Barbara Walters forge to the front and remain there. Such a drive, though, can produce negative outcomes in the form of dictatorships and gangs.

Those people who have sharpened the **Builder** part of themselves created the financial empires of Wall Street, London, Tokyo and Toronto. They are the industrial giants of mass production, the super businesses of financial prosperity, national organized education and the structured charitable institutions of parental service on the community level. The **Builder** sets up the organized, structured assembly line that practically and sensibly pushes out products by the zillions. They are the advocates of the organizational person whether political, financial, or religious. Look for the **Builder** aspects of your work environment. Why do you need a CEO? Why do you need middle management? What is authority like? Does the management staff always sit behind a desk when speaking or interviewing you? Are results the exclusive focus of your work place or organization rather than you as a person?

- Watch the video/film <u>Patton</u>. Even though, at times, the personality is exaggerated, it serves as an excellent example. Compare the personalities of President Reagan and former President Nixon who were both **Builders**. Reagan had a strong **Relater** backup and surrounded himself with **Planners**. On the other hand, Nixon was closer to a pure **Builder** and primarily surrounded himself with other **Builders**. Watch an old re-run of <u>Star Trek</u> or <u>Star Trek: The Next Generation</u>. Note the **Builder/Relater/Planner** qualities of Captain Kirk or Jean-Luc Picard. Watch Voyager and Janeway in the role of **Builder** captain. There are so many marvelous videos such as <u>White Night,</u> <u>Breakfast Club,</u> <u>Lion In The Winter,</u> <u>The Twisted Cross</u>, and <u>Winston Churchill</u> (Man of the Century). <u>Law and Order</u> is another excellent series for examing several **Builders**. Read about Elizabeth I, Watergate, Cattlegate or the Korean Airline incident and you will find the strong hand of the **Builder** present in the final evaluative decisions.

- Examine the procedures of Kenneth Starr and his function as an independent prosecutor using the Grand Jury investigation of President Clinton. How did his **Builder** persona serve him testifying before the House Impeachment Committee? How did he use his backup **Planner** strength?

___

- Can you think of any experiences you have had with a **Builder** either in the workplace or in the community? What happened?

___

Strategy for Developing/Working with Persons with this Behavior.

If you desire to organize and order your life for success, observe and seek the assistance of **Builders**. As Aristotle observed: *"The first function of a wise person is to put things in order."* Ask a **Builder** how to best obtain the job or project you want, how your current job might be a steppingstone to future financial success and how you might advance in it.

- Visit a local courtroom and observe the **Builder** atmosphere. Why do you think the **Builder** atmosphere is nurtured and maintained in such a setting?

___

- Think back on the trial of O.J. Simpson. What roles did Johnny Cochran, Barry Scheck, Christopher Dardin, Marsha Clark and Judge Lance Ito play? Why?

___

- What were the motivational strengths of witnesses Fred Goldman, Mark Fuhrman and O.J. Simpson?

___

- If you lack information on the O.J. Simpson trial, read some of the published books. <u>In Contempt</u> by Christopher Darden with Jess Walter offers **a Planner's** perspective of the trial.

- If you have difficulty organizing your ideas into a concise format, list them and consult with a **Builder**.

Do You Have This Behavior? How to Use It to Your Advantage.

If you are a **Builder**, be aware of the possible exception to every rule. A tendency to organize and establish a pattern and continue in the same way may have strong benefits, but may prevent your ability to see the uniqueness of a given situation or person. Don't get into a rut! It is said that a rut is a coffin with the ends kicked out!

As a **Builder,** list practical ways to develop an open attitude.
_____
_____
_____

My Career Connection: I will have a job that allows me to develop and demonstrate being in charge.

Your Personal Empowerment Statement: I have a sense of progress as I proceed towards my goal (name it in vivid terms). Inch-by-inch, it's a cinch.

Bottom line It!

Lee Iacocca

Bottom Line It!

Builders want results. They do not like it when you beat around the bush. "What is it you want? Get to the point!" is their response when you give vague or unclear requests. If you insist on giving numerous details or base your requests on a purely humanitarian basis, you will have little chance of being heard. They want a concise one-page report! **Builders** love a challenge and if they are negative, will demand every drop of blood. Challenge the integrity of a person with strong **Builder** behaviors and you are finished unless you are equally as powerful!

Iacocca revitalized Chrysler Corporation with Builder concrete steps that attained results. Notice how successfully using the same means, he headed the committee for repairing the Statue of Liberty. Look at how Ross Perot, with a no nonsense approach, changed the whole political thrust of the 1992 presidential elections. Hillary Clinton is another example of **Builder** behaviors in action.

- Give a sample of a bottom line response to a **Builder** superior's request.

- How would a Builder bottom line respond to another person's complaint?

- How did Hillary Clinton, as the President's wife, demonstrate the strengths of a **Builder**? Evaluate her proposed national health care program and her book, It Takes A Village: And Other Lessons Children Teach Us.

Strategy for Developing/Working with Persons with this Behavior.

Before approaching any **Builder**, make a clear outline of what you want. Boil it down to the bare essentials. Present your request in an organized step-by-step fashion. For example, if you are applying for a job and the interviewer is a **Builder**, make sure you have a well-organized resume and are able to express exactly what you want. State your qualities and how you will be able to contribute to the profit and success of the company or organization. If you are asking for an evaluation of a presentation from an employer or a client who is a **Builder**, be concise and balanced. Give short, precise answers on exams if they are given (or written) by a **Builder**.

- If you have a general resume and it is not precise, revise it before presenting it to a **Builder** interviewer.

Do You Have This Behavior? How to Use It to Your Advantage.

Your tendency for the bottom line may make you appear cold and unconcerned about people. If you do not temper your communication with warmth, you will drive people away. Compare the personality of President Reagan, Hillary Clinton, Margaret Thatcher or General Swarzkopf with that of General Patton or F. Lee Bailey. You may defeat the possibility of obtaining successful results if you relate only with the **Builder** part of yourself.

- Consider President Clinton's address to the nation after the investigation of the Monica Lewinsky affair by Kenneth Starr. What were the costs of delivering it solely in a **Builder** style?

  _____
  _____
  _____

- How was his follow-up, whole person apology accepted?

  _____
  _____

- How far do you think the entire incident would have gone, if from the beginning President Clinton had taken a Builder approach? What do you think the response would have been, in January of 1998, if he had told the truth and apologized **Builder/Relater** style?

  _____
  _____
  _____

- How would a **Builder** using **Relater** overtones respond to a complaint?

  _____
  _____
  _____

My Career Connection: I will have a job that allows me to get my work done efficiently.

Your Personal Empowerment Statement: When I choose, I bottom line my position (graphically) in a powerful, direct, concise and friendly way.

Color Me Traditional

Born in the USA

Tradition and patriotism are part and parcel of the **Builders'** way of life. Whether it is rebuilding a national monument, like Iacocca, the investigation process of Watergate/Irangate or Whitewater, **Builders** always champion traditional causes and national pride. They give strong support to businesses, schools and local traditions.

Builders are extremely status conscious. Respect should be given to one's elders and authority. That respect must be gained through a tradition of hard work, responsibility and accountability to the home, school, business and nation.

- Think about the words of the National Anthem. Why is it a **Builder** song? Can you think of any other songs that have this theme, e.g., "God Bless America", "The Green Berets", "Born In The USA"?

- What has been the response to the bombing of embassies by the people and the governments involved?

- How would a **Builder** react to acts of terrorism?

- How would a **Relater** differ in his or her response to acts of terrorism?

- What would be the reaction of a **Planner** to acts of terrorism?

- How would an **Adventurer** react to acts of terrorism?

- Why are talk show hosts, such as Rush Limbaugh and G. Gordon Liddy, so successful? Do they use a **Builder** conservative approach?

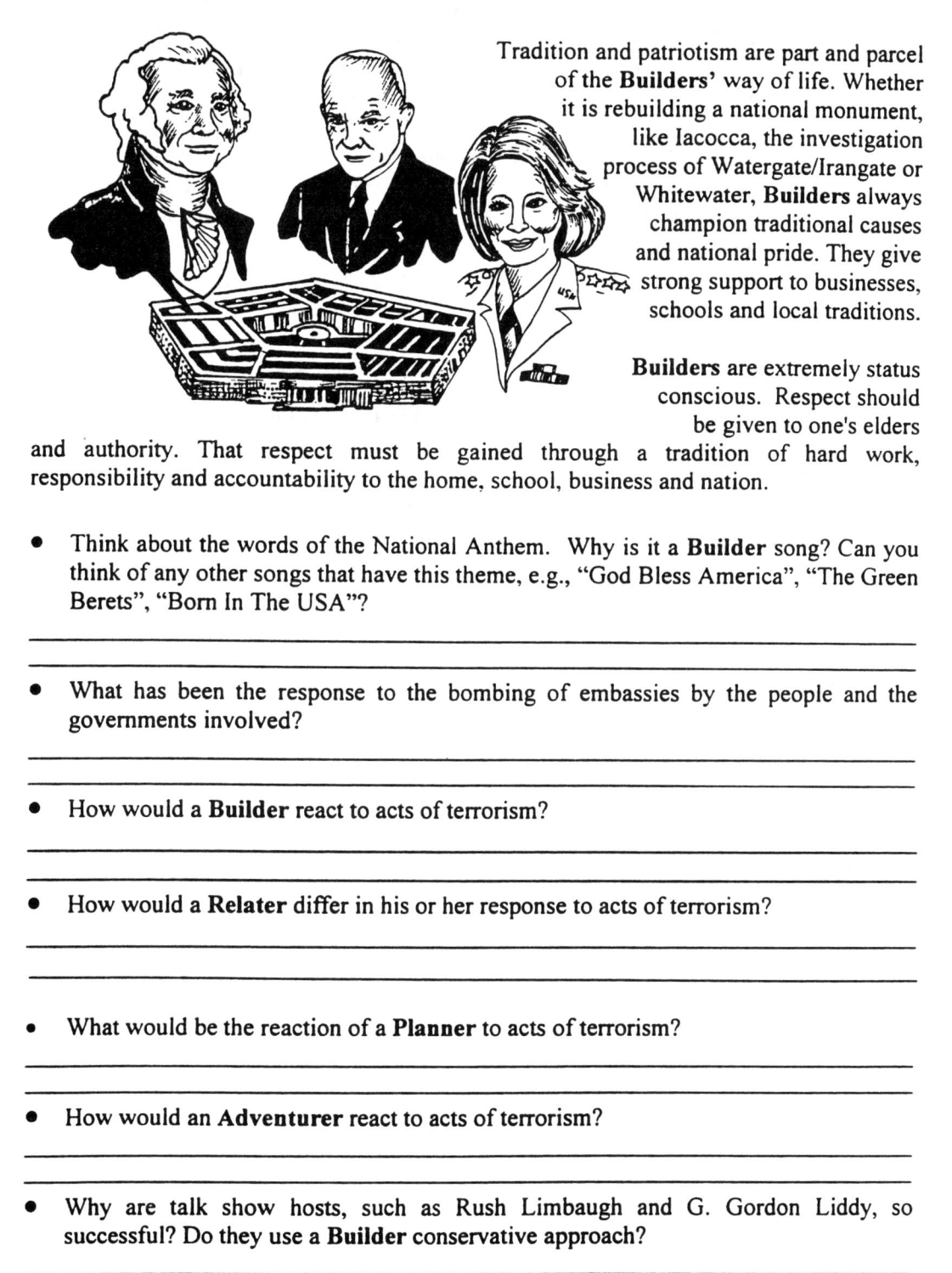

Strategy for Developing/Working with Persons with this Behavior.

Be aware of the traditions a particular **Builder** you know has invested in over the years. What are the family, school, community, company, or organizational values of a **Builder**? If you wish to remain on the **Builder's** good side, recognition of his/her titles and due respect for his/her age and accomplishments is crucial.

- List several corporate/organizational traditions. List several local and national traditions. What are the pros and cons of such traditions? Note the power of tradition. What happens when a tradition or symbol is violated by someone who has no respect for another's customs, e.g., flag burning?

Do You Have This Behavior? How to Use It to Your Advantage.

Your emphasis on tradition may block out possible progress. Always ask yourself if this new idea may strengthen the bottom line results you wish to attain.

- List traditions in education that promote and those that may hinder progress. For example what is the effect on learning when people sit in rows? How does the standing instructor affect his or her relationship with those learning?

- Can you identify nations trying to assume the role of **Builders**? President Slobodan Milosevic and his Serb forces who purged Kosovo of ethnic Albanians or Pakistan and the leadership of Benazir Bhutto would be examples.

My Career Connection: I will have a job that allows me to work in an environment that respects traditional values.

Your Personal Empowerment Statement: I have a deep appreciation of those who have gone before me (name) and the freedom (specify) they have given me.

Color Me Powerful

Towering Inferno

Builders want power. They proceed toward their goals with passionate enthusiasm. There is no second rung, only the top of the ladder. They want the best home, club, team and business. They want to be in full command regardless of the outcome. Remember the force and drive of Reagan who came out swinging after the attempted assassination on him. If one recognizes the **Builder** behavioral cluster of taking a hard line, Hillary Clinton's reactions to the White House crisis are understandable. This characteristic is also exhibited in Madeleine Albright, Janet Reno, Queen Elizabeth, General Schwarzkopf and Margaret Thatcher.

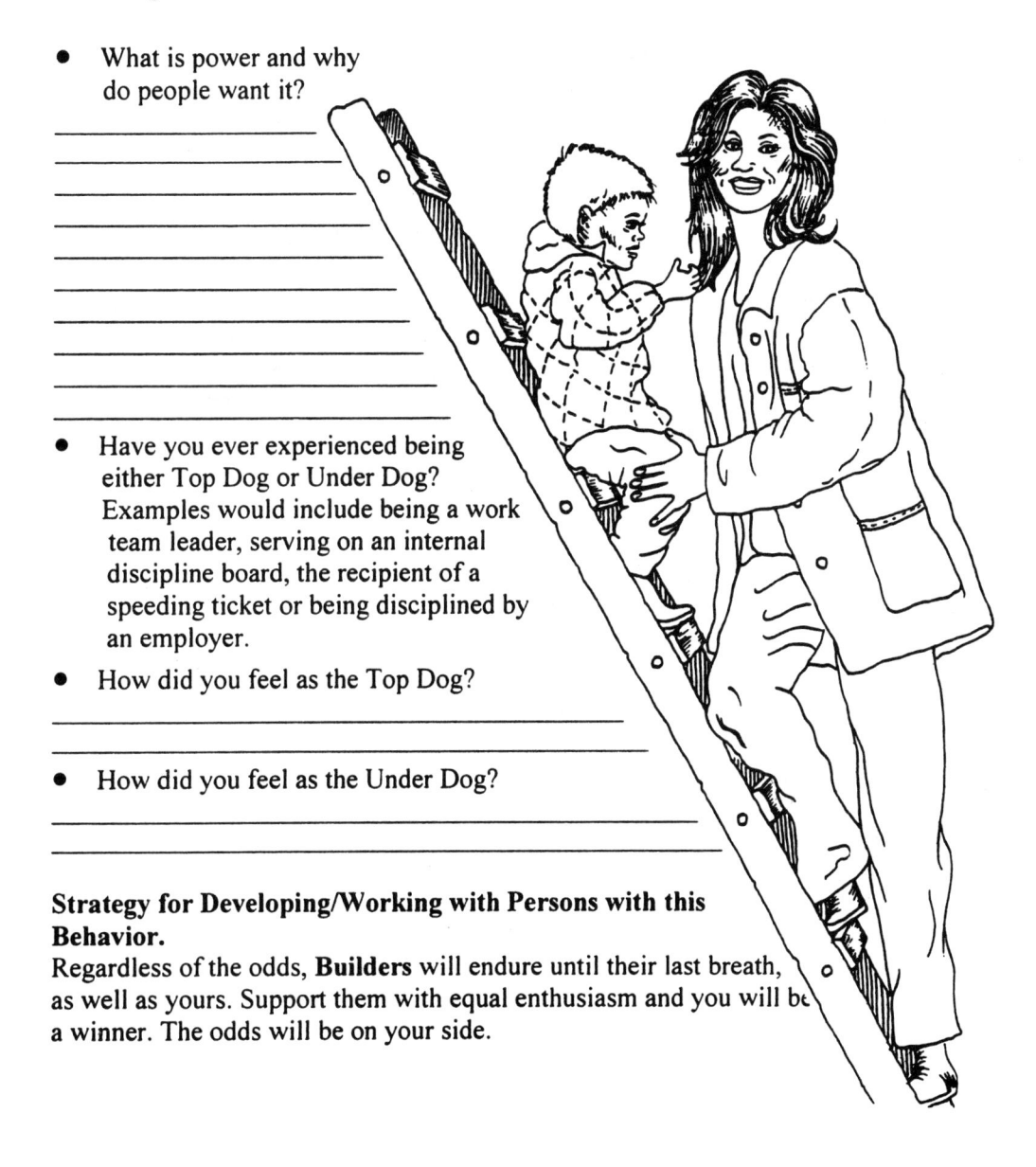

- What is power and why do people want it?
  _____
  _____
  _____
  _____
  _____
  _____
  _____

- Have you ever experienced being either Top Dog or Under Dog? Examples would include being a work team leader, serving on an internal discipline board, the recipient of a speeding ticket or being disciplined by an employer.

- How did you feel as the Top Dog?
  _____
  _____

- How did you feel as the Under Dog?
  _____
  _____

Strategy for Developing/Working with Persons with this Behavior.

Regardless of the odds, **Builders** will endure until their last breath, as well as yours. Support them with equal enthusiasm and you will be a winner. The odds will be on your side.

If they have negative or destructive goals, take care, they may use or walk over you to get what they want (Saddam Hussein or Osama bin Laden). Don't become a pawn in their chess game (Stalin)!

Show gratitude and appreciation for their service. They deserve it.

Give them a challenge or goal that allows them elbowroom and visible signs of accomplishment.

- Write out situations in which you have felt pressured and overpowered by a **Builder**.
  _____
  _____

- With your understanding and awareness of **Winning Colors**®, what strategy would you use the next time you are feeling pressured and overpowered by a **Builder**?
  _____
  _____

Do You Have This Behavior? How to Use It to Your Advantage.

If the basis of your power is fear, those under your thumb will be looking for the opportunity to escape. When they do escape your power, watch out. Read the history of Mussolini and his death at the hands of the Italian people he had ruled. Follow the news regarding the former USSR, Palestine, Serbia, Croatia, Bosnia, Kosovo or South Africa. These are all hotbeds for continuing revolution.

- How can newspapers, magazine articles and television reports plant seeds of fear? Think about serial murders/nuclear threats/AIDS. Do newspapers, magazines or television ever abuse their power?
  _____
  _____

My Career Connection: I will have a job that allows me to satisfy my ambitions through the force of my personality.

Your Personal Empowerment Statement: I temper my ambition with understanding and caring for myself and others (name).

Color Me Result-Oriented

Madeleine Albright and Janet Reno

Builders want bottom line results! They take quick action to get the results they want. If they act on sufficient information, they quickly attain the desired end. Notice the differences between the actions taken by Ronald Reagan, a **Builder**, in Libya/Granada and Jimmy Carter, a **Relater**, dealing with the Iran hostage situation. Margaret Thatcher, the former Prime Minister of Great Britain, is known as the "Iron Lady." Her overwhelming victory in the Falkland Islands quickly and effectively gained the desired results. Argentina learned, as did Kaddafi with Reagan, it was not wise to cross the "Iron Lady." Consider the positions taken by Janet Reno as Attorney General. They want to see visible results.

- Crisis situations: A person is alone on a darkened street. Another person approaches and pulls out a knife. What would be the **Builder's** behavioral response?

- What would your response be to the above situation?

- Watch the film <u>Hunt for Red October</u> and analyze how each of the sub captains dealt with the several crises.
- Compare in your mind the public handling of crises by President Bush and President Clinton.

Strategy for Developing/Working with Persons with this Behavior.

Unless you are prepared to produce, you will not be on the best of terms with **Builders**. **Builders** will look for the results whenever they deal with you as an employee, family member or even a friend. The business or organizational world is interested in IF IT WORKS, not the theories explaining why. A clear, concise, printed report impresses a **Builder** superior.

- If you have access to the video **Winning Colors**®, review the section on hostage negotiations. If there is a J.R.O.T.C. program in your local high school, they will probably have this video.
- How would you handle an assignment given to you by a **Builder**?

- What are the "Production" expectations of your **Builder** employer/CEO?

Do You Have This Behavior? How to Use It to Your Advantage.

If you make the Journey along the way so miserable for those involved, you may drive away the same people who might have helped you attain results. Study and seek the advice of **Relaters**. Look at the successes of General Swarzkopf, General Colin Powell (Planner/Builder) and Vice President Dick Cheney (Planner/Builder) opposed to the failures of General George Patton, in the area of public relations.

- How would a **Planner** advise a **Builder**?
_____
_____

Was the advice practical, bottom line and not a sermon? Did you, while playing the role of a **Planner,** give hands-on steps so the **Builder** might not drive away team members?

My Career Connection: I will hold a job that allows me the freedom to focus on the results without distractions.

Your Personal Empowerment Statement: When I choose, I relish visible tangible results (name them).

GO FOR THE GOLD
JACKIE JOINER KERSEE

Color Me Decisive

Decisiveness

One of the excellent qualities of **Builders** is their ability to make decisions. Results cannot be obtained unless there is a commitment to act. Examine the leadership of Golda Meir of Israel.

If you wish to become a salesperson, you will appreciate the **Builder** buyer who will give a quick response to purchasing your product. You will always know where the **Builder** stands. You may not like the **Builder's** position, but you will not be kept in the dark. If they lower the wall, there will be no information forthcoming. When G. Gordon Liddy said, "No comment," he meant it and stonewalled all the way to prison, through prison, through his parole and into the role of a radio talk show host.

- Complete the exercise on the following page "So How Do You Make Decisions?" What did you learn about yourself, your family members, friends and peers?

_____
_____

How Do You Make Decisions?

For most of us, we learned our decision making style from those around us as we were growing up. Our models may have been parents, siblings, teachers, ministers, employers, peers or the school of hard knocks. How do you make a decision?
Place a check in those boxes most like you.

How do your friends, fellow employees or family members make decisions? You can either write their initials after the type of decision or you might make copies of this form and have them complete it.

This is a good resource for mentoring helpers to refer to when helping someone.

Are there other decision making styles you can add to the list?

☐ Don't make the decision.
  By not making a decision it happens by default.

☐ Don't make the decision as it may upset the apple cart.
  Let someone else decide and then he or she is responsible.

☐ Make a decision because it is expected.
  A formal structure has designated who will make the decision.

☐ Make only a portion of the decision now.
  Piece meal decision making.

☐ Make a decision expecting it to end the process.
  Never look-back-decision making.

- ☐ Make a decision because it feels right.
    Emotionally based decisions.

- ☐ Let fate make the decision.
    Assumes fate is on your side.

- ☐ "Starlight, star bright . . . I wish I may, I wish I might . . .
    Doesn't take into account that the star one is wishing on may be a satellite.

- ☐ Defer the decision.
    "Let Mikey do it!"

- ☐ Won't make a decision because it will open me to criticism.
    Hidey-hole (hiding in the closet) decision making. Decisions are made in order to please.

- ☐ I just don't know, making this decision could hurt someone, then again maybe . . .
    The agonizing decision making style.

- ☐ I will make the decision, but reserve the right to change my mind.
    The "don't pin me down" decision making.

- ☐ I need more time to think before I can make a decision.
    The "old and you'll be gray" decision making. Contemplate until the decision dies.

- ☐ I need much more information before I make a decision.
    The cautious decision maker. Bury the entire process in detail.

- ☐ What decision do you think I should make?
    The easily influenced decision maker who wants to defer responsibility.

- ☐ Just make the decision, get it over and move on.
    The expediting decision maker.

- ☐ What do we have to lose making the decision now?
    The risk-taking decision maker.

- ☐ OK, Sounds good to me.
    The impulsive decision maker.

- ☐ What is the big deal? Make a decision.
    The relaxed decision maker.

- ☐ I'll make the decision and you will live with it.
    The aggressive decision maker.

- ☐ I take responsibility for the decision.
    The self-directed decision maker.

My decision making style:
_____
_____
_____

- The Decision-Making Process. See the completed sample for working with a younger person and blank form following "How Do You Make a Decision?" page. Practice using this form yourself before you use it to help a friend or co-worker. Select a problem/challenge. Work your way through the process. Refer back to the completed example if you have questions. You are now ready to use the process with a friend.

When using the Decision Making Form, you will serve as the recorder while the other person presents the challenge. It is crucial that three options be listed, but the recorder never suggests which option is better. To do so, relieves the person of the challenge of all the responsibility for his or her choice and actions. The positive (+) and negative (-) consequences of each option are given and recorded objectively by you. In the role of recorder, you may suggest options or overlooked consequences, but not show preference.

Psychologically, the placing of the pros and cons of the option in each of the ovals gives credence to the idea that the challenge is manageable. After completion, the person with the challenge selects one option.

The form is also great to use for individual and group brainstorming sessions.

Remember the steps for decisiveness include: perception, association, evaluation, decision. Also note that not deciding is a decision.

THE DECISION FORUM

THE DECISION MAKING PROCESS

The Challenge: Living at home has become intolerable

Option 1
Remain at home

Positive Consequences +
+ Free rent/a roof
+ Free food
+ Can last seven months until the end of school year

Negative Consequences -
- Constant arguments
- Drinking & Battering
- I have become an enabler
- No privacy
- Can't study/grades dropping

Option 2
Move in with friend's family

Positive Consequences +
+ Support/understanding
+ Stable family
+ Will be able to study
+ No costs involved
+ Care about me
+ Can finish school/degree
+ Same neighborhood

Negative Consequences -
- No privacy/share a room
- No income/feel like freeloader
- My family may harass my friend's family

Option 3
Quit school and get a job

Positive Consequences +
+ Can earn money for an apt./car
+ Can get out of a bad situation
+ Eventual privacy
+ Can earn a GED

Negative Consequences -
- No degree
- Costly to set up house keeping
- No dental, medical or car insurance
- May not be allowed to see brother & sister

Do I Need More Information?

My Decision

Colors I Need to Bring Up

86

THE DECISION MAKING PROCESS

The Challenge:

Option 1
- Positive Consequences +
- Negative Consequences −

Option 2
- Positive Consequences +
- Negative Consequences −

Option 3
- Positive Consequences +
- Negative Consequences −

Do I Need More Information?

My Decision

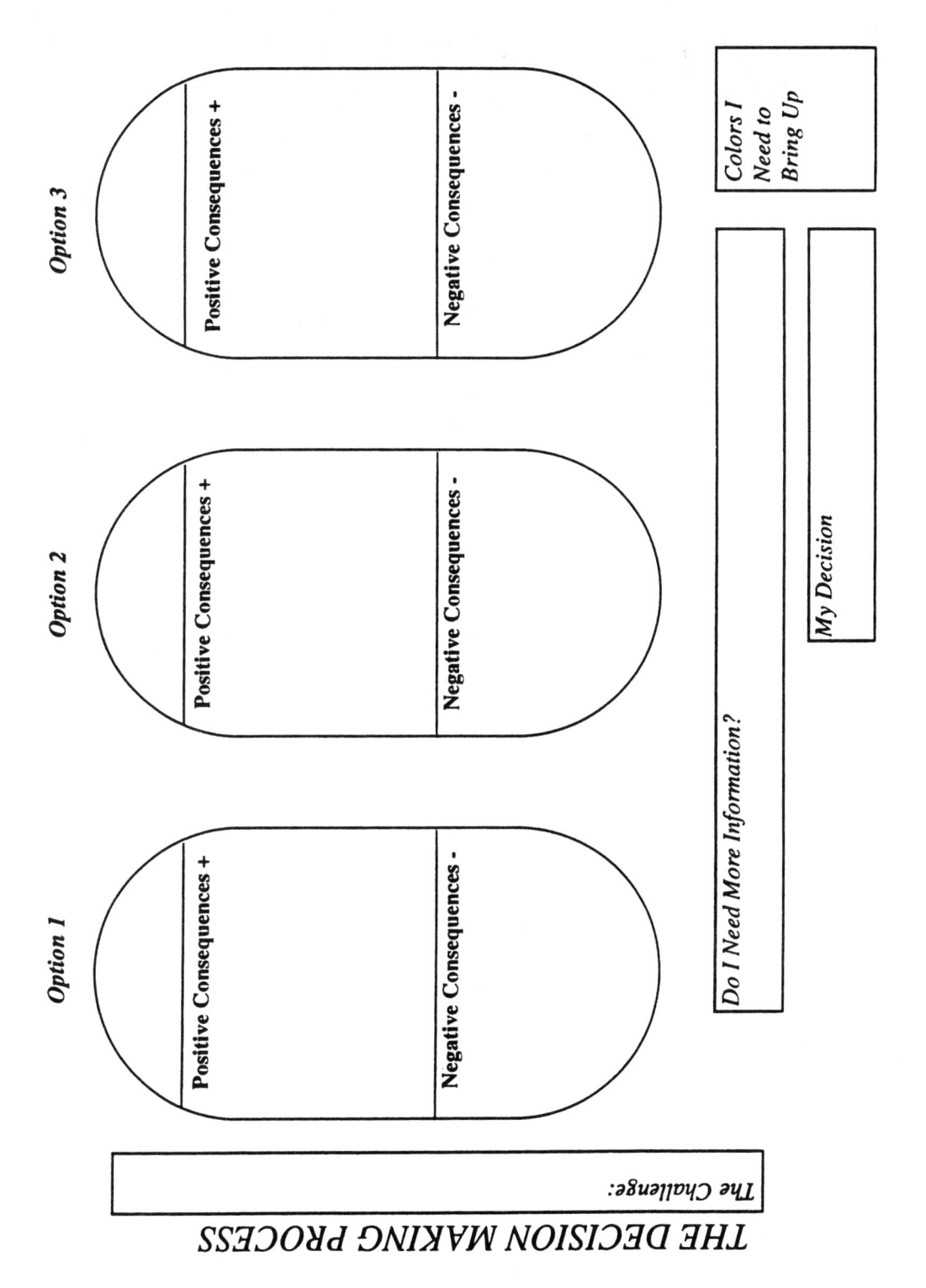

Colors I Need to Bring Up

Strategy for Developing/Working with Persons with this Behavior.

You will usually have only one shot at making a presentation to a **Builder**. Make sure it is bottom line, result-oriented, traditional, and clear. Maintain eye contact. Never look down. Place yourself physically on the same level, e. g.; if the **Builder** stands, you stand. Shake hands firmly. This is particularly important for a woman.

Do You Have This Behavior? How to Use It to Your Advantage.

Make sure you have sufficient information before making your decisions. It would be wise to have **Planners** give you input before making any serious commitment. They see the depth and breadth of problems and proposals. As a leader you will see the value of working with a variety of personalities on your team as opposed to cloning. Consider Dwight Eisenhower's following remarks on leadership:

> ". . . Leadership is a word and a concept that has been more argued than almost any other I know . . . I would rather try to persuade a man to go along, because once I have persuaded him he will stick. If I scare him, he will stay just as long as he is scared, and then will be gone."

Eisenhower was not suggesting cloning when he used the term persuade. What he was suggesting was the open give and take dialogue for which he was known. Surround yourself with like strengths and in the end you will be weakened.

- How would a **Builder** get information from a **Planner** in a non-threatening way?

_____
_____
_____

Think about the pros and cons of cloning. Consider the future of society and the scientific possibility of cloning: Aldous Huxley's Brave New World or the movie The Boys from Brazil can serve as resources.

- What do you think would be the impact of a **Builder** dominated society?

_____
_____
_____
_____

My Career Connection: I will hold a job that allows me to have the authority to make decisions.

Your Personal Empowerment Statement: I have a sense of fulfillment and potency as I review the pros and cons of three options (name them) and choose and act on the best (name).

Color Me Paying My Dues

Battle of the Alamo

Builders will endure and fight until they've spilled the last drop of their blood or yours. In the film <u>Patton,</u> the soldiers remarked as he passed by, "There goes old blood and guts! Our blood and his guts!" Pain and sacrifice are necessary elements in life. The good life must be both earned and defended. They consider painful struggle a challenge. Value is never gained by freeloading. Greater love than this has no man, than to give up his life for the good of his country or fellow man.

- As the world moves toward a leisure society, how do you think a **Builder** might adapt?

_____

- How would you compare the work ethic with the leisure ethic?

_____

- If you haven't done so yet, watch the film <u>Dead Poet's Society</u>, <u>Apocalypse Now</u>, <u>The Gladiator</u> (Adventurer/Builder) or the television series, <u>The Sopranos</u>. Examine the **Builder's** attitude to duty, tradition and sacrifice.

Strategy for Developing/Working with Persons with this Behavior.

If you are to join their ranks, you may be assured that sacrifices similar to those they impose on themselves will be demanded of you. Whether long hours or unquestioned obedience, if circumstance demands it, you will be expected to oblige. On the battlefield, orders will be given to achieve the objective. If there is remorse, it will be after the fact, if at all. You simply play the odds, knowing they are in your favor if a **Builder** is with you. The organizational structure of the military is an exact fit for the **Builder**. Rules are to be followed. Objectives are to be achieved. Their leadership is not to be questioned. Individuals are expected to conform.

Consider the builder qualities of your instructors, employers and managers. Adjust your style accordingly. Take the **Builder** motto of the Boy Scouts to heart: "Be Prepared!"

You will want to have such a person in your group, for he or she will be a constant source of inspiration, as well as perspiration. They will motivate the group to be successful. As long as they are not abusive, any service club, business, organization, or meeting should have a **Builder** involved. If success is possible, it will be attained. If it is impossible, you have a chance.

If you join a group that has a **Builder** as the leader, do not expect to exit the ranks with ease. If you cross or betray him/her, you will pay the price. It will be heavy and harsh. You do not cross the Mafia. The Nazi Gestapo was a negative **Builder** Gang!

- List below the benefits and costs of belonging to exclusive clubs or groups. Discuss hazing activities in educational institutions and the price paid by some for belonging (their life).

Benefits:
_____
_____
_____
_____

Costs:
_____
_____
_____
_____

Do You Have This Behavior? How to Use It to Your Advantage.

Be aware that others respect you for your courage and endurance. As vocalized by a top newspaperman when speaking of a particular leader of a nation: "I hate his guts, but I respect him!"

Other people may not come up to your rigorous standards. Nurture whatever degree of courage you find in others. Even though they may not be as courageous as you, it is better to have at least part of this quality. Take care or you may, by your insensitivity, wipe out even this portion. Through tolerance and patience, you will be able to increase their courage.

Builder, the key to your success lies in your being able to see yourself as a coach, a nurturer of champions! What do you perceive to be the differences between a coach and a dictator?

Coach:
_____
_____

Dictator:
_____
_____

My Career Connection: I will hold a job that allows me to work my way to the top and be rewarded for my efforts.

Your Personal Empowerment Statement: I am strong and capable of persisting in reaching my goal (name it).

Color Me Dutiful

Saving Private Ryan

The character played by Tom Hanks, in Saving Private Ryan, possesses a sense of duty that drives him to fulfill orders regardless of the consequences to himself or his command. Orders are orders and are not to be questioned.

No drive is more powerful than that which carries **Builders** to their goals. They work with a passionate excitement, especially when opposed. Opposition strengthens the flow of their adrenaline. Patton told his troops quite bluntly, "We do not hold our position! It is the enemy who holds their position. We advance!" President Bush, and particularly General Schwarzkopf's, handling of Iraq were done in true **Builder** style.

Children will not receive the same exterior emotional affection that they would from the **Relater** parent. They may even think that their Builder father or mother doesn't love them, especially if the other parent is visibly affectionate. It isn't that such a parent does not care, but that the parent cares in a practical, sensible, dutiful and responsible way.

The **Builder** is comfortable with the hierarchical organizational structure vs. the horizontal organizational structure using Quality Circles. The horizontal line of authority is democratic by nature, e.g., the person in charge bases his/her decision on the input of everyone involved.

- Emotions flare quickly, whereas passions have a more enduring quality. Think about the passionate love of Romeo and Juliet. Watch the film Romeo and Juliet in terms of **Relaters** surviving in a pure **Builder** Society. Compare this film to Dead Poet's Society. Read The Charge of the Light Brigade focusing on the line "Into the valley of death rode the six hundred".

Strategy for Developing/Working with Persons with this Behavior.

Do not mistake the **Builders'** apparent lack of exterior emotion as passivity. They have a powerful underlying drive toward establishing the good life through constant effort and work. Evaluate your level of strength before joining their ranks.

- Give examples from life, books, television and movies of passionate drives, e.g., Barbara Jordan, Senator Orrin G. Hatch, former governor of Texas Anne Richards, Ted Turner, Douglas MacArthur, Captain Ahab of <u>Moby Dick</u>, <u>The Organization Man</u>, Alexander, Eleanor of Acquataine, <u>Law and Order</u>. List them below.

_____
_____

Do You Have This Behavior? How to Use It to Your Advantage.

Learn to temper your steel! That is how you become stronger! Let your power inspire rather than discourage. You are able to handle the ocean storms with ease. Your challenge is to evaluate the level of strength of those about you. It isn't wise to send ducks to eagle school! Allow others to progress from the stream, to the river, to riding the roaring waves with you.

Respect the fact that some persons may neither care nor have the capacity to live beyond the challenges of a stream, e.g., leaders are in for a surprise if they expect followers to put in the same free overtime that they demand from themselves. Read the history of the Mars family for a fascinating study of such expectations and the end result.

- Write out a strategy of how Builders could take their teams from the stream to the river to the ocean waves. Start with the work place or a service organization and proceed to clubs and other live situations.

_____
_____
_____

My Career Connection: I will hold a job that allows me to work in an environment where duty is valued.

Your Personal Empowerment Statement: I passionately take those steps to reach my goal (name it).

Color Me Responsible

Rock of Gibraltar

According to the skill and intellectual level, **Builders** will generally follow through. They are usually stable and dependable. It will be a job well done.

- Watch some films of John Wayne such as True Grit to illustrate this personality trait.

Strategy for Developing/Working with Persons with this Behavior.

Delegate the task according to the person's capabilities, then relax, it will be completed. Don't stand over his/her shoulder!

- Think about situations and the capabilities required for the job, e.g., a service organization or a coaching position.
- When a Builder is out of control and acts like a bully rolling over everything in his or her path, we describe this behavior as clouting. Saddam Hussein of Iraq would serve as such an example. How might a bully succeed in gaining the leadership position, yet not have the people skills to lead well?

Do You Have This Behavior? How to Use It to Your Advantage.

Remember that feelings are important in being successful. It would be well for you to seek out the counsel of **Relaters** as a check on how you are coming across to the public, e.g., Patton receiving counsel from Bradley, "The Soldier's General."

- What are the differences between authority and feelings?

Authority	Feelings

How do you assist the **Builder** in becoming balanced in this area?

My Career Connection: I will hold a job that allows me to take on all I can handle.

Your Personal Empowerment Statement: Like a solid rock, I take a stand (name it) and allow new information to guide and change my drive to success.

Color Me Leading

Zeus

Builders want to lead. There is an actual thirst for power and control. **Builders**, parental by nature, are born to rule. They feel responsible for establishing an ordered society. Those **Builders** who rule well will establish a group, home, business, or nation that will function smoothly, efficiently, and predictably. The history of the British Empire is an example. The beginning of their undoing occurred when they did not monitor the types of colonists that they allowed to immigrate to America.

Did you, as a child, ever play the old game "Mother, May I?" It gave the participants a feeling of power, control and submission. In the game, players must ask "mother," the **Builder**, permission for every action they take, e.g., "May I take 10 giant steps?" The mother **Builder** may grant or refuse. The participants must always say, "May I?". It is a child's game that provides first hand experience in a hierarchical based organization.

Strategy for Developing/Working with Persons with this Behavior.

Make sure **Builders** receive sufficient information to balance their decisions. The higher the position, the greater the need for keeping them well-informed. You may need to develop creative ways of getting new information to **Builders**.

- List below several creative ways you might employ to convey new information to a **Builder**:

  _____
  _____
  _____

Sometimes, they are quite certain they know everything. Never tell them face-to-face they are wrong, especially in front of others.

- A **Builder** employee is not up to standards. What information should be taken into consideration by the manager in assessing the person's capacity for improvement?

  _____
  _____

- How should the employer/manager handle the situation?

  _____
  _____

Do You Have This Behavior? How to Use It to Your Advantage.

Builder, make certain that you have a staff of unbiased information givers who will not just follow you out of fear. It would be well for you to have a couple of **Planners** close at hand, e.g., Nixon supported himself with a mixture of **Builders** and **Planners** on his staff during his first term. During his second term, he surrounded himself with **Builders** and **Adventurers**. The only **Planner** of any significance on his staff was John Dean. The Watergate scandal resulted in Nixon's resignation. The powerful person is the one who has the capacity to listen, compare the new information with the old, make judgments based on the information and is able to delegate. The successful leader is the one who incorporates all four strengths.

- To be an effective communicator, you need to continually practice the gathering or listening process as a means of getting objective information. When you are the listener repeat what you hear, not your reaction to the material. Your feedback should be in 3 dimensions: words, emotions, pictures. The next time you have the opportunity to practice this process, record the results and your impressions on the lines below.

___

___

My Career Connection: I will incorporate all four strengths in my leadership on the job.

Your Personal Empowerment Statement: I feel a sense of authority as I take on leadership in the situation (name it) in which I am fully competent to lead successfully.

I make progress by having people around who are smarter than I am – and listening to them. And I assume that everyone is smarter about something than I am.
        - Henry J. Kaiser

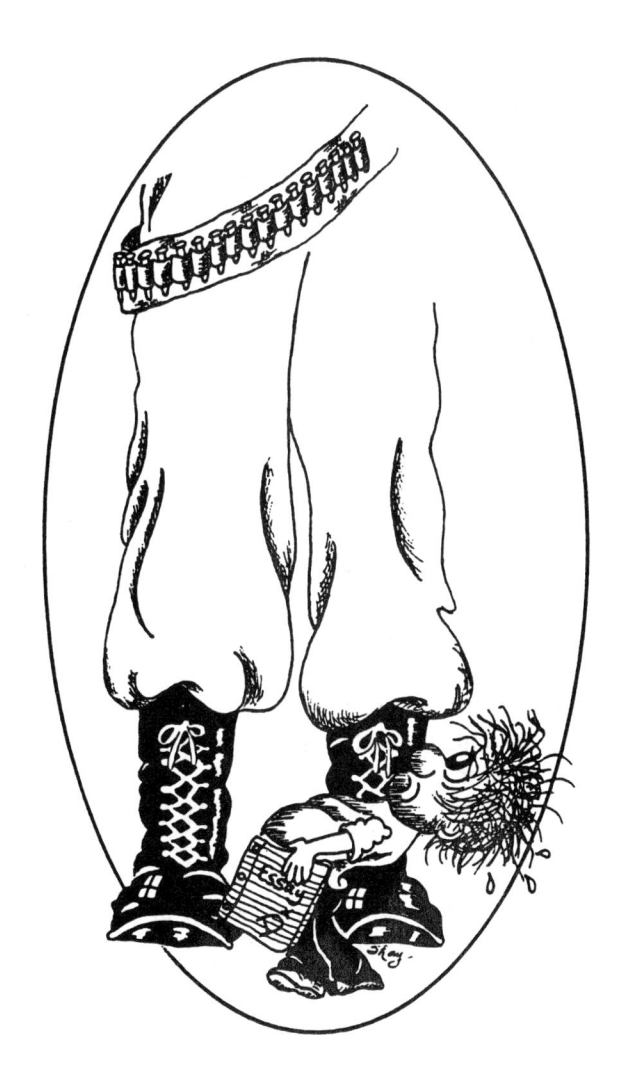

Color Me Controlling

Caretakers of Humankind

Builders are the caretakers of humankind in a class, team, club, family, corporation or nation. They feel obligated to carry the load. **Builders** find no challenge in delegating work, but do have difficulty in delegating their authority.

This difficulty to delegate any authority may stop the educational process in others in the learning stages, an employee, a friend or a smaller brother or sister. All creativity may come to a halt. The seeds of hostility may be sown. **Builders** may alienate themselves from others unconsciously and be left alone. They will feel unappreciated by others for their sacrifices made for family, friends or country. History illustrates this in General MacArthur's powerful speech concluding with the statement: "Old soldiers never die! They just fade away!"

- What does it mean to delegate?

  _____
  _____

- Think of instances in your own daily experiences when you have delegated. Perhaps your immediate supervisor asks you to prepare a liabilities assessment report. You, in turn, ask your staff to gather the raw statistics. This is an example of delegating. When school students are in a cooperative learning group, tasks and responsibilities are delegated to individual members. Why is delegation important with younger children in our culture? How was it done in former days? Although a vintage television show, watch <u>Little House on the Prairie</u>. Compare the farm children to the store children.

  _____
  _____
  _____

Strategy for Developing/Working with Persons with this Behavior.

Once the reins are in the **Builder's** control, they are absolutely certain that they alone can direct and accomplish the task with the most efficiency. At an early age, the child with **Builder** tendencies should be shown the value of allowing peers to "do their thing!" Builder parents think this should be done in a dutiful and responsible way, so they would say: "By acting in this manner, you will gain the respect of others and attain what you wish. People will want to follow you. Try it and see."

Builders are concerned about having their power usurped, whether in the work place, on a pilot program, in a service group or at home. Support them rather than challenge their authority. The son or daughter, no matter what his or her age, who mistakenly challenges the **Builder** is in for certain defeat and perhaps, in some cases, a continuous battle. This is especially true if the parent lacks self-knowledge and does not temper their need for authority under control.

- How do you feel when presenting a position you are heavily invested in, or when you meet resistance in the form of negative body language? What if the person listening to you continually shakes his or her head, folds legs or arms and seems distracted? Does such a reaction impact your presentation?

- Based on what you have learned so far in *Winning Colors®* what should you do? Modify?

Do You Have This Behavior? How to Use It to Your Advantage.
Recognize that if you delegate authority, you will develop responsible people and increase the number you command. You will also increase your authority. You will be able to concentrate on the bottom line. You will receive a sense of appreciation. Bees are attracted by honey, not vinegar.

Make a list of advantages for delegating authority that would appeal to a **Builder**.

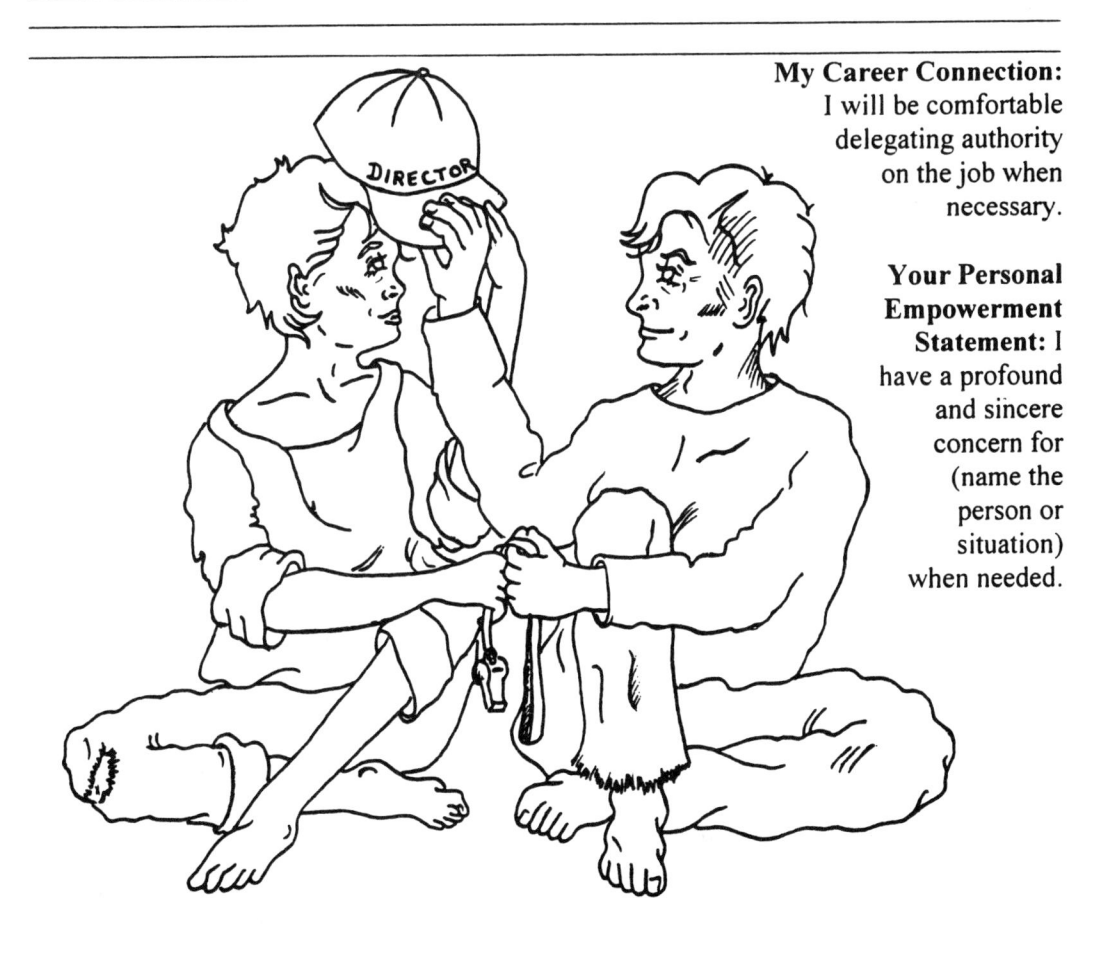

My Career Connection: I will be comfortable delegating authority on the job when necessary.

Your Personal Empowerment Statement: I have a profound and sincere concern for (name the person or situation) when needed.

Color Me Committed

Builder of the American Dream

Builders believe in earning the right to lead by being vigilant, steadfast, faithful and committed. Patton thought it was his duty to protect the moral rights of the American people. He was a warlord and conqueror as were the ancient warriors of old. He was convinced he had received ingratitude and lack of appreciation for the service he had so faithfully given his country. His lack of diplomacy and the press' magnification of this flaw brought about his dismissal as one of the major leaders of the Allied Command. It was not the diplomatic thing to do, to broadcast the danger of Russian domination, when in fact they were an ally!

- Make a list of several people and situations in which **Builders** consider it their duty to protect the rights of their religion, politics or people, e.g., MOSAD, John Adams, Lincoln, Anwar Sadat, Manachon Begin, Lewis Farrakahn, Pope Paul, Attorney-General John Ashcroft.

_____
_____

Strategy for Developing/Working with Persons with this Behavior.

Make sure their dream is in keeping with your own value system and your dream. Do not expect them to adapt their dream to yours.

- Think about this statement: "Go West Young Man, Go West!" Is there an escape from reality in the American Dream? What about the people who have fled to the suburbs in order to escape crime? Have they discovered the American Dream or have they brought crime with them?

_____
_____

Do You Have This Behavior? How to Use It to Your Advantage.

You will lose all power if people abandon you. People may be part of a lead or pilot team for different reasons. For example, one may join for the experience, another because of personal interest, another for reasons of ego/status, and still another for office politics. Allow your team members to fulfill their motivations. It is said of Jonathan Swift, of <u>Gulliver's Travels</u> fame, that only his housekeeper and cat attended his final satirical sermons, which attacked a decadent society. Finally, we are told that only his cat survived. Act accordingly.

- What are some of the different reasons why people would like to be on the same team, e.g., a basketball team where one of the advantages may be exercise, or fame or money?

_____
_____

My Career Connection: On any job I hold I will be goal focused.

Your Personal Empowerment Statement: I am vigilant, steadfast, faithful and committed to obtaining (name the goal such as a particular behavior which needs to be reinforced or acquired).

The Adult Builder in Summary

You were born to lead. A car seat that faced backwards was not for you. Seeing where you had been was boring. You wanted to see where you were going. You were not particularly impressed with the concept of sharing. All you surveyed in the world was yours. If one of your sandbox buddies had a toy you wanted, you went for it. Stair and room gates, child-proof spinning door knobs and yardsticks threaded through drawer handles were viewed as barriers to be conquered. Things put up on shelves, out of reach, served as challenges. Crawling took time, walking was more efficient. When you were being read to from your favorite books, you closely monitored for any omissions. There was an order to your toy box. Tricycles were great because you could move even faster. And then you spotted a bike. You immediately wanted to "buy up." The bike arrived but it came with training wheels. How mortifying! The removal of them became paramount. You were already setting goals. No videos were to be taken until you were master of your two wheels. One of your favorite characters on Sesame Street was Miss Piggy. She knew what she wanted and she usually got it. "Etch-a-Sketch" didn't make sense to you. Why spend all that time creating something just to have it erased in a single shake? You were the first kid on your block to open a lemonade stand. You immediately understood profit and loss. Profit was yours. Loss was for your competitors. If they priced their lemonade at 10 cents you answered by lowering your price to 9 cents. Lucy in Charlie Brown was your example of an entrepreneur. The game of Monopoly was more fun to you than Clue or card games. It provided you the opportunity to practice your financial skills.

If you had older siblings in your life, you focused on catching up to them. You followed them like a shadow. Any attempts to shake you off were met with either resistance or the offer to negotiate. What was it worth to them? At a young age you understood the importance of being cool. You learned early that showing your emotions could be a display of weakness. Elementary school was fascinating. Finally you had a chance to observe all the behavior colors in one place. You didn't know what you were doing, but you recognized that different styles and approaches achieved different ends. Some of your classmates talked all the time. Some classmates couldn't sit still. Others were the reticent classmates, the watchers. Finally there was a small group like yourself. You felt most comfortable around them. You liked tasks that allowed you to be in charge such as collecting papers, writing names on the board or taking roll. Unlike the **Adventurers,** you put your gold stars on the citizenship board in a neat straight row.

CEO
REPRESENTATIVE
SENATOR
PRESIDENT

Middle school was a training ground for developing leadership skills. You preferred the role of captain rather than waiting to be selected. Winning was important, losing was for the other team. The political scene opened up to you with the electing of class officers. You were always amazed when a **Relater** or an **Adventurer** beat you out for an office. It was time to refer to your notes from elementary school about the styles of the other colors. Apparently the skills of relating and being adventurous were appealing. You refined your skills in preparation for high school.

High school was a time for setting serious goals. Being a leader was a motivating drive within you. A number of you entered the political arena and ran for office. When you included the elements of the Relater, Adventurer and Planner into your campaign, you were more successful.

Being in front of a group, large or small, was a comfort zone for you. You enjoyed making presentations. Confidence was your game. Learning for you was serious business. You were competitive. Being the best at whatever you did was important. You understood the logic behind team projects and cooperative groups, but members who either slapped their contributions together or didn't complete them, drove you crazy. Today, these qualities are still an integral part of you.

Friends are important to you. You do not gather them in great numbers like a **Relater**. That has never been your style. Quality over quantity is your motivational operandi. Your friends know they can count on you. Attending a formal dance in high school was an event to be well organized and programmed. As an adult, you still believe waiting until the last minute is foolish. You began the on going process of putting your resumes and applications in order while in high school. Graduation for you was not so much a goal as it was a stepping block to either advanced vocational training or higher education.

When Uncle Sam said, "I Want You!", it was you he wanted. <u>Leadership, duty and honor are motivational forces within you.</u> As General H. Norman Schwarzkopf, you served as the Commander in Chief of the United States Central Command from 1988 to 1991. When Iraq invaded Kuwait your command responded with the largest deployment since the Vietnam War. The success of Operation Desert Shield and Operation Desert Storm became signposts in what former President George Bush called the beginning of a new era of internationalism. Upon your retirement you received the Presidential Medal of

Freedom. Your balance of colors made you special as a military leader. The following quote by you is a reflection of that balance.

"The mothers and fathers of America will give you their sons and daughters . . . with the confidence in you that you will not needlessly waste their lives.
That's the burden the mantle of leadership places upon you.
You could be the person who gives the orders that will bring about the deaths of thousands and thousands of young men and women.
It is an awesome responsibility. You cannot fail.
  You dare not fail . . ."

As Major General Claudia J. Kennedy, when you were nominated to become a Lieutenant General, you became the Army's first female officer to wear three stars. A press release noting your beginnings as a cryptologist said you had "broken the code" in obtaining a three-star rank for female army generals. You joined ranks with Navy Vice Admiral Patricia Tracey and Marine Corps Lieutenant General Carol A. Mutter.

The world of publishing is not for the fainthearted but it is for **Builders** like yourself. You will thrive in an environment where deadlines are a constant. Whether a daily newspaper, a weekly publication or a monthly magazine, the presses either roll on time or nothing reaches the stands. Most of us are reminded of the Hearst Castle when we hear the name Hearst. It took 28 years to create. The estate consists of 165 rooms, furnished with Spanish and Italian antiques and art, located on 127 acres of gardens and terraces. It truly is a status symbol, evidence of achievement and a reflection of the late William Randolph Hearst. At the age of 23, Hearst assumed leadership of the *San Francisco Examiner* entering the world of publishing. By the 1920's he owned a chain of newspapers from coast to coast. One in four Americans read a Hearst Newspaper. He experimented with all aspects of newspaper publishing. As a **Builder** he was innovative using multiple-color presses, halftone photographs on newsprint, comic sections in color and wire syndication of news copies. What we know today as the UPI evolved out of the Hearst International News Service. Today Hearst Newspapers consists of twelve daily newspapers.

The original philosophy of William Randolph Hearst remains a guiding force.
  "We must be alarmingly enterprising,
  and we must be startlingly original . . .
  and do new and striking things
  which constitute a revolution."

When one hears the name Ted Turner, Turner Broadcasting comes to mind. Turn on the television, begin surfing channels and you will encounter Ted Turner. Turner Broadcasting System, Inc. is the major supplier of entertainment and news programming in the world. As a **Builder** his contributions in the communications industry are legendary. His risk-taking as an **Adventurer** is apparent in his programming. What most people do not see are his **Planner** and **Relater** sides. Quoting from *Tribute 21:*

> In 1985, he launched the Goodwill Games and, collaborating with the former Soviet Union, organized the quadrennial, multi-sport, international, world-class competition. He is a member of the Board of Directors for the Martin Luther King Center for Nonviolent Change, the Greater Yellowstone Coalition, and for the International Founders Council of the Smithsonian Museum of the American Indian. Turner is also President of the Turner Foundation, Inc., a private grant-making organization focusing on population and the environment. Mr. Turner has received numerous civic and industry awards, including being named <u>Time</u> magazine's Man of the Year in 1991.
>
> "The Turner Foundation, Inc. dedicates itself to environmental preservation by promoting natural resource conservation, wildlife protection and sound population policy. It lends support to educational efforts to instill in all citizens a sense of responsibility for the fate of the planet. The Turner Foundation is strongly committed to preventing damage to natural systems and to innovative institutions working to protect these systems. Its grant-making efforts go primarily toward environment and population-oriented programs."

The following quote upon becoming a recipient of *Tribute 21* reflects Turner's motivational operandi:

> *"My main concern is to be a benefit to the world, to build up a global communications system that helps humanity to come together, to control population, to stop the arms race, to preserve our environment."*

Your enjoyment of public recognition, combined with your ability to present in a confident manner and think on your feet, makes you a candidate for public broadcasting. The public seems to prefer **Builders** in the positions of news broadcasting. Four different **Builder** styles of delivery can be found in Ted Koppel, Diane Sawyer, Tom Brokaw and Greta Van Sustern, Peter Jennings and Christianne Amanpour (Adventurer back up).

<u>You have a sense of the land, a respect for it, whether tilling, ranching or developing it</u>. You will take as much pride in a small farm as the 15,500 acres of the King Ranch. Do **Builders** have the vision of **Planners**? Read about Captain Richard King, founder of the King Ranch. Today this ranch is considered by many to be the birthplace of the American ranching industry. It was on this ranch that the Santa Gertrudis, the first beef breed in the United States, was developed in 1920. A second breed, the King Ranch Santa Cruz, was developed as the result of the collaboration of the ranch staff and twenty-six professors

from fourteen universities. In addition to beef, the ranch has been the producer of some of the all-time top performance horses. The ranch has entwined technology with the agricultural business world and energy development. Land reclamation projects including wetlands, marshlands and river control will also call upon your **Builder** vision and innovation.

Your respect for law and order makes a career in law enforcement a natural for you. Authoritativeness is a part of your make-up. There are rules to be followed. There is a classical hierarchy in law enforcement with clear levels of responsibility. It provides you with a visible position in the community. If you are **Builder** with a red back-up, you enjoy the continuous change in daily work and the risk factor involved. If **Planner** is your back-up color, investigative and detective work appeals to you. Legal professions are closely linked to law and order. Your ability to present in a confident and concise manner makes you a formidable force in the courtroom as an attorney or on the bench.

Discipline is an integral part of your value system. It is a foundation that provides the basis for stability and order. It is necessary in reaching your goals. It will serve you well if you opt for a career as a professional athlete. The most decorated Winter Olympian in American history, Bonnie Blair, is such an example. She is the recipient of five gold medals, the most won by an American woman in any sport. She has consecutively broken records in the 500 and 1000 meter speed skating competitions. Felissimo, in awarding her the Tribute 21 Award said, "She is celebrated for producing her best performances when it counts most." What is her philosophy?

> *"I wish to teach others the joy I have experienced. Sports combines dedication and personal discipline and is simply the best way I know to bring people together."*

Challenge is a strong motivational force within you. The field of medicine affords the **Builder** the continual mental challenge of being current in both research and surgical techniques. Your ability to make rapid on site decisions in surgery is a critical strength. If you enter family medicine, consulting, pediatrics or geriatrics, it will be important to develop your **Relater** skills. The **Planner** part of you will be on constant call to see what is not seen by others. Perhaps the best known physicians in the United States have been Doctor Spock and former U.S. Surgeon General C. Everett Koop (1981-89). Dr. Spock's Baby and Child Care became a bible to millions of mothers worldwide.

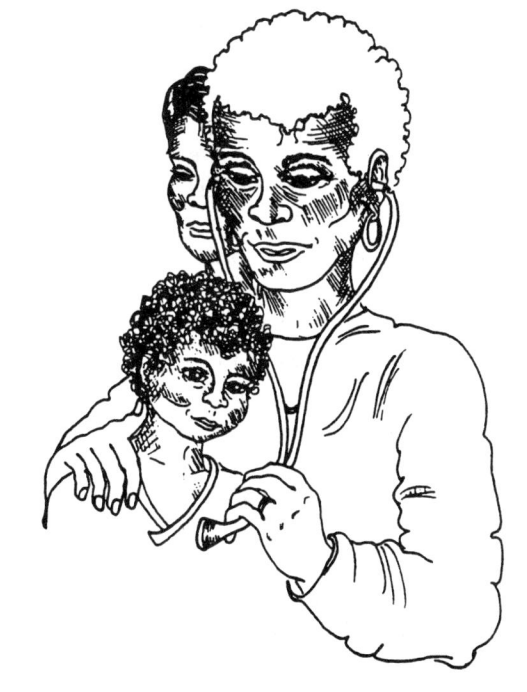

We all knew where Koop stood on the issues of public health, from smoking to AIDS. He never beat around the bush. To educate Americans on AIDS, he sent out 107 million copies (the largest mailing in U.S. history) of a brochure titled "Understanding AIDS: A Message from the Surgeon General." His position on tobacco as addictive angered the tobacco industry. His non-judgmental position on AIDS incensed the conservative right. His response to the criticism was, " . . . controversy comes with the job." In 1998 at the age of 80 he spoke out against doctor assisted suicide. When asked about retirement he summed up his position:

> *"The idea that you have to retire at 65 is nonsense.*
> *People who think that retirement should be a time*
> *for hobbies and traveling are deluding themselves.*
> *They'll become sluggish."*

Builders do not retire, they just change jobs and their focus.

Your ability to see the big picture is an asset. In fact, you prefer the big picture over minutia. You recognize the value of detail, but would prefer to have others do the collecting and then reduce it to a maximum of five major points.

Money is a vehicle to achieving your goals. To you, the world of finances is a battlefield to be conquered and controlled. The careers of banking, investment, securities and brokerage will provide you the opportunity to enter this battleground.

In your opinion, negotiation and mediation are art forms if accompanied by power. You are a natural policy maker. Examine careers in foreign affairs and diplomacy. Read <u>The Wise Men</u> by Walter Isaacson and Evan Thomas. It is an in-depth examination of the lives of William Averell Harriman, Robert Abercrombie Lovett, Dean Gooderman Acheson, John Jay McCloy, George Frost Kennan and Charles Eustis Bohlen. Quoting Isaacson and Thomas:

"Out of duty and desire, they heeded the call to public service. They were the original brightest and best, men whose outsized personalities and forceful actions brought order to the postwar chaos and left a legacy that dominates American policy to this day… During the 1940's, they authored a doctrine of containment and forged an array of alliances that, for better or worse, have been the foundation of American policy ever since. Later when much of what they stood for appeared to be sinking in the mire of Vietnam, they were summoned for their steady counsel and dubbed 'the Wise Men'."

The closing line of The Wise Men states, "In their sense of duty and shared wisdom, they found the force to shape the world." Beginning in 1997, it became the responsibility of Madeline Albright, the first female Secretary of State and the highest ranking woman in the U.S. government, to continue carrying this policy forward.

Lester Brown is the founder of the World Watch Institute. He has been described by the *Washington Post* as "one of the world's most influential thinkers." As a **Planner** he has been a driving force in shaping the global environmental movement. So what is he doing in the **Builder** section? Many years ago this author began using Brown's *World Watch Institute* publications in her history classes because they were on the cutting edge. This writer was impressed by Brown's ability to take subjects like world population, malnutrition/starvation, and nuclear energy and compress them into manageable formats for readers. It quickly became apparent he was taking a **Builder** bottom-line approach. He instinctively knew the only way he was going to get the attention of the drivers, movers and statesmen was to be succinct and concise and use **Builder** language. Go to the library or web and check out his prolific writings He is the author of a dozen books in addition to co-authoring a number of books, articles and pamphlets.

Elizabeth Dole as a **Builder** began her advocacy work beginning in 1968 under the administration of Lyndon B. Johnson when she took a job in the Office of Consumer Affairs. During Nixon's administration she was appointed to a seven-year term as a member of the non-partisan Federal Trade Commission. She is the only woman to serve as a Cabinet Secretary for two different federal departments. In 1991, she assumed the role of President of the Red Cross. As the wife of Bob Dole, she took a prominent role in his 1997 campaign. Though he lost, it served as a visible political platform for her. In 1999 she entered the presidential primaries. Lack of financial funding forced her to withdraw. It would not be a surprise to see her continue to be a political force in the 2002 or 2008 elections. See Parade Magazine, September 27, 1998 for a list of 19 other female 21st century potential candidates.

Politics is an arena where **Builders** thrive. Businesses, the professions and the political arena, historically have been dominated by men. As women in greater numbers enter these arenas, they will need to seek a fine balance. Men by default have and are, rightly or wrongly designated as **Builders**. Women by contrast must earn the designation through merit. Not everyone is greeting this change with an open mind. Often when women assume **Builder** roles, negative descriptors are attached to them. No one remembers a strong monarch from history being designated the "Virgin" King or a Prime Minister being referred to as "The Iron Man." If you want to have some fun research the secret service code names given to the wives of U.S. Presidents. It quickly becomes apparent which wives chose to maintain a low profile and those who elected to step forward. Know there is now a women's bathroom for women Senators. Prior to 1992 there was no such facility.

You are motivated to lead. The back or the middle of the pack is not for you. You will be drawn to the arena of politics. Consider the person in the U.S. Presidency spot. It's a good day when 55% of the population agrees with you. The other 45%, perhaps fifty to seventy million, will disagree with you. It takes a strong **Builder** to enjoy a political career. Check out the careers of Senator Kay Bailey Hutchison, Representative Barbara Jordan (recipient of The Freedom Medal), Senator Trent Lott, Senator Tom Daschle. Certainly examine your own U.S. Senators and Representatives and determine who are the **Builders**.

The **Builder** in you will be most damaged by failure, because it damages so many of your values. You value success, being in control, status and recognition. When confronted with failure, get out a copy of <u>Built To Last</u> by James C. Collins and Jerry I. Porras. Read up on the story of Johnson and Johnson. Children's casts dyed with pure food color that bled out on bedding, failed ventures in heart valves, kidney dialysis and ibuprofen pain relievers have all been a part of their history. Yet in 107 years they never posted a loss. Quoting Collins and Porras, "In reality, J & J's history is filled with favorable accidents, trial and error, and periodic failures. Summed up Chief Executive Ralph Larsen in 1992: Growth is a gambler's game." J & J kept their corporate **Builder** balanced with **Adventurer** and **Planner**.

Relater and **Planner** are reflected in Collins' and Porras' comment on the 3M Company: "Although the invention of the Post-it® note might have been somewhat accidental, the creation of the 3M environment that allowed it was anything but an accident."

When you or those around you fail, it will take balance, courage and strength on your part to carry forward. Hillary Rodham Clinton serves as an example to all those who followed the Monica Lewinsky affair. Enough said.

If the arts appeal to you, explore the **Builder** scale of Henry Moore and Christo. There are no limits.

In closing consider the following two haikus:

Builders, architects
Of empires, families
Keepers of the flame
---Shay

To not give one's best
Is beyond comprehension
Why enter the race?
---Shay

Your Communication Key (Decide and Lead):

Build a down-to-earth, traditional atmosphere

Your secret vocabulary for:

♦ developing Builder behaviors

♦ getting along with persons with strong **Builder** behaviors:

* organized * law and order * power * saving * results * honor *

* track record * duty * responsibility * accountability * bottom-line *

* prepared * building * clear-cut * authority * leading * status *

BUILDER - BROWN

Build down-to-earth, traditional atmosphere

Comfort zone: Orderly; structured procedures at work, home, school, social, recreation; pride in organization, school, family; preference for input and procedures that have a solid, traditional stable foundation; importance of discipline, routine; desk in position of authority; conservative dress and hair styles; everything must indicate status, e. g., home, family, clubs.

Demands on people: Duty conscious; obedient, respect, success oriented, hard working, reliable, prepared, responsible; able to finish projects and assignments within time limits; reports must be neat, concise and on time.

How to build powerful teams, self-esteem, success, maximum productivity in others and reinforce leadership

* HOT BUTTONS *

When the **Builder (brown) part of self** in a person is very strong, consider what motivates that person and apply it.

- Take a bottom-line approach to **Builders'** communication.
- Be duty conscious and comfortable with rules and directions.
- Allow accountable and responsible positions according to talents.
- Explain directions in a step-by-step, concrete fashion.
- Treat in the right and proper way.
- Give them status or control over people or things according to their people skills.
- Have a concrete reward system.
- Establish a stable, structured, home/social/work situation.
- Let them know what is expected of them.
- Establish daily routines and give step by step, concrete explanations.
- Never embarrass or cause them to lose face in front of their peers.

How I Find Out About The Relater Part of Me

Some Observable Behaviors with Exercises for Developing Them

Color Me A People Person

Color Me a Relater

Persons with **Relater** behaviors are people centered. Their warmth makes you feel wanted. They show you they care. One of the greatest examples of the twentieth century was encased in the small diminutive body of Mother Theresa. Her entire life revolved around caring for the less fortunate of India and making them feel truly loved. On the other side of the world Diana Princess of Wales, whose back up strength was that of a **Relater**, impacted the lives of so many people from different walks of life - victims of AIDS/HIV, land mines, struggling artists or poverty.

Relaters temper the sternness of the **Builder**, the seriousness of the **Planner** and the playfulness of the **Adventurer**. Anyone who has seen Robin Williams and Whoopie Goldberg (primary strength is **Adventurer**), Bill Cosby, Billy Crystal, Gilda Radner and Howie Mandel perform, understands this talent for tempering the strengths of others and teaching them to laugh at themselves. They have the skill to make everyone feel at home and at harmony in the group. They like to join clubs, be in discussion groups, and socialize. Persons with **Relater** behaviors are attracted to groups that offer an opportunity for deeper experiential relationships.

Remember, we have all four clusters of behavior. Some people have developed the **Relater** part of ourselves more than the others. The mature person has the capacity to bring up these four clusters of behavior according to the situation. Jackie Joiner Kersee, who grew up in the inner city, despite enormous odds, became a world wide class athlete. She is a marvelous example of such balance. A **Builder** will set his/her goals and never waver in his/her training journey. She set a standard in her field. She believed firmly in having a plan and stated on a number of occasions that mental preparation (**Planner**) was an integral part of her training and success. The **Adventurer** in her allowed no room for limits. When she left the arena of competition, she was a six-time Olympic Medal winner. Today the **Relater** in her is concentrating full time on her foundation efforts to improve life for the kids on East Street.

- Practice smiling versus not smiling while talking on the phone. Test the effect on the same person calling several times. Explain to the friend what you are doing. Log the calls with the smile and those without the smile. Ask the friend if he or she was able to tell the difference?

Strategy for Developing/Working with Persons with this Behavior.

With training, **Relaters** make excellent arbitrators. They equalize the static filled air. Scott Hamilton, former men's world champion and international professional skater, has been recognized for his ability to bring together the many diverse personalities of his fellow skaters on tour with <u>Stars on Ice</u>.

- The next time you are involved in a conflict, bring up your **Relater** skills when you seek resolution. Remember to use the power words of a **Relater**. According to the situation, arbitrate conflicts as a **Planner, Builder** or **Adventurer**. Assess your results.

Observe various disagreements between an immediate supervisor and staff person, an employee vs. an employee or parent and child. Take note of how different colors handle conflict.

Do You Have This Behavior? How to Use It to Your Advantage.

Relaters beware of the group you want to join. Check it out! It may be a group with a leader like Jim Jones, which resulted in the mass deaths by suicide in Ghana. Read the history of Neville Chamberlain who came back to England waving a treaty of peace that he had just signed with Hitler. He exclaimed "Peace In Our Time!" which was really "Peace At Any Cost!"

- Are there any local groups or service organizations that **Relaters** would be enticed to join? List them below and the reason they would appeal to a **Relater**.
_____
_____
_____
_____
_____

- On your job, as a part of a team or in a service organization, how could you reinforce the self-esteem of your peers?
_____
_____
_____
_____
_____

My Career Connection: I will have a job that allows me to interact extensively with my co-workers.

Your Personal Empowerment Statement: I feel a sense of comfort in being warm and gentle to (name or situation).

Color Me Caring

A Rescuer in Case of Flat Tires

Those with **Relater** behaviors are very giving and are quick to come to the rescue of anyone in need. They will be the first to approach those who have had an accident. They will stop, when no one else will, if you are out of gas. Your best chance of help will usually come from a **Relater**. Accordingly, **Relaters** will dispense their acts of kindness in a friendly and warm way. You will feel that, rather than putting them out, you are actually doing them a favor by allowing them to help you. In contrast, **Builders** may perform the same act in a rather cold, forthright manner, while **Planners** will do it in a concerned and understanding way. Relationships are the lifeblood of **Relaters**.

- Take on a **Relater** challenge. Commit to one act of kindness each day for one week. On the 7th day do an act of kindness for yourself. Your act of kindness can be as simple as covering someone's phone for an hour, doing a room mate's chore or leaving a short supportive note for a spouse or friend on their desk. Leave a post-a-note as your marker with a smiley face, the sign of the phantom or whatever symbol works for you in a family member's lunch sack. Plan or develop a plan for your acts of kindness on the lines below. Record your feelings at the end of the week.

	Person	Act of kindness
Day # 1		
Day # 2		
Day # 3		
Day # 4		
Day # 5		
Day #6		
Day # 7 (Do an act of kindness for yourself.)		

After a week of completing 7 acts of kindness, what are you feeling? What were the reactions of the recipients?

- Take a couple of minutes and write your life history.

Make a list of those things you like about yourself.

- Of these two exercises, which was the easiest for you to complete? Why?

Strategy for Developing/Working with Persons with this Behavior.

If you are working with **Relaters**, make sure you provide occasions for them to be helpful. This will develop and refine their self-esteem while at the same time fulfill their need to be wanted.

- Make a list of five people who you are close with in your life. Identify one small need each has that you might supply.

    Name   Need

1. _____

2. _____

3. _____

4. _____

5. _____

Do You Have This Behavior? How to Use It to Your Advantage.

Develop and take pride in your gift for responding to the needs of your fellow human beings. Learn how to say "No" when needed. As you know, sometimes people take advantage of your good-hearted nature. If you are exploited, you will be too burdened and be of little help to anyone.

- Why should you and others take pride in possessing the gift of responding to the needs of your fellow human beings?

_____
_____
_____
_____

My Career Connection: I will give back to my community as a part of whatever career I select.

Your Personal Empowerment Statement: I feel super terrific when I choose to help (name or situation) in need.

Color Me Feeling

A Little Learning is a Dangerous Thing

Relaters are usually concerned with feelings, emotion or the exterior reaction. Consequently they sometimes miss what is going on behind the scenes. Their objective judgment sometimes becomes clouded because of emotional entanglement. They become so occupied with the quarter of the pie that they miss the whole pie. "A little learning is a dangerous thing. Drink deep or taste not of the Pierian Spring!"

- Generally, since their actions are based on feelings, new interests and opportunities will capture their attention. What they usually want is light work rather than manual labor. They want to attract a lot of attention. They love the burst and flare of fireworks. Deep continuous thought is not for them unless their emotions are involved. They are the keepers of the warmth of the hearth.

- The next time you are in a group of people or on the job, take a few minutes and observe those around you. Mentally guess what each person is feeling. The focus of this exercise is to develop keen observation skills.

- What do you think is the concept behind the People Watcher's List? (page 26)

_____
_____
_____

Strategy for Developing/Working with Persons with this Behavior.

Be cautious of advice or suggestions given by the **Relater**. It may be from the emotional level rather than the practical. **Relaters** have a good grasp of exterior detail, but often miss what lies below the surface.

- Can you think of any situations in which a superficial suggestion may be harmful, e.g., use of drugs, diets, work short cuts?

_____
_____
_____

Do You Have This Behavior? How to Use It to Your Advantage.

Make sure you have the viewpoints of others that are not **Relaters** before taking action on important matters. Above all, take an in-depth course concerning active, empathic listening. Check with a **Planner**.

My Career Connection: On the job/in my career I will practice empathic listening skills.

Your Personal Empowerment Statement: I always consider situations (name) from a thinking point of view as well as feeling.

Color Me Super Positive

A Cock-eyed Optimist

We live in an age of increased skepticism and cynicism Yet, it is refreshing to have persons who view the pitfalls of life as eventually and inevitably, leveling out into harmony. **Relaters** love and genuinely care for people. People are the center of their lives.

The challenge, of course, is that **Relaters** have an inclination to become emotionally entangled. In these relationships, there is a tendency to over exaggerate the emotional exchange of the moment. Consequently, they become involved in relationships first and secondly question the wisdom of their choices. <u>The Bridges Of Madison County</u> by Robert James Waller is an excellent example of this tendency.

- Think of a negative situation in your life. Be brief and concise and sum it up on the lines below:

___
___
___

- Now describe the above negative situations in a positive way.

___
___
___

Strategy for Developing/Working with Persons with this Behavior.

In any essential decision making, check out the facts and don't fall victim to the **Relaters'** positive emotions that may hide the obstacles. They love making grandiose plans and decisions based on *emotion* rather than possibilities. They act on an intuitive feeling level. Has emotion overpowered the clarity of the intuition? Be well aware that their fantastic plans may have many loopholes and the decisions may not be the best. There may be times when they make poor decisions. There are two types of **Relaters** - those who see the glass half-full and those who see the glass half-empty.

- What are the pros and cons of intuitive decision making?

___
___
___
___

- Have you ever been caught in grandiose plans? What happened?

___
___
___
___

It is not the grandiose plans that one should avoid, but the lack of a Plan of Action to bring such plans to fruition.

Do You Have This Behavior? How to Use It to Your Advantage.
Happy, positive people are cherished. Practice the People Watcher's Form, (page 27) so that you may become adept at picking up the signals of your misplaced emotion. Ask **Planners** to give you feedback as to when you are getting on people's nerves without being aware of it.

- What are the costs of gossiping and discussing the weaknesses of others?
  _____
  _____
  _____

- Do you think there should be any limits on the press regarding privacy?
  _____
  _____
  _____

- Examine why people are drawn to cliques. What are the costs?
  _____
  _____
  _____

- Do you think some talk shows are nothing more than gossip sessions?
  _____
  _____
  _____

- Why do you think some people are drawn to paper and television tabloids?
  _____
  _____
  _____

My Career Connection:
I will have a job that allows me to work for and with positive people.

Your Personal Empowerment Statement: I am excited by possibilities such as (name).

Color Me Romantic

Sentimental Me, Guess I'll Always Be!

Relaters are romantics at heart. They search out opportunities to be completely open and honest. An emotional intimacy is a must in any relationship. Authors like Danielle Steel and Jackie Collins and the writing team of Judith Barnard and Michael Fain, known as Judith Michael, understand the power of romance and possess the formula for consistently having their books on the Best Seller List. Such writers provide a venue for romance where anyone can participate by simply picking up one of their novels. The next time you are in a bookstore or in front of a book display, take note of the space occupied by Gothic romances. The numbers speak for themselves. Romance is alive and well.

- What are the pros and cons of being honest and open?
  _____
  _____
  _____

- Do you always want complete honesty? Why or Why not?
  _____
  _____
  _____

- Think about such phrases as "How are you?" Why do you think most people will say "fine!" even when they feel terrible?
  _____
  _____
  _____

Want to find out if people are truly listening to you? The next time someone asks you how you are doing, quietly give a negative response. Did he/she respond appropriately?

Strategy for Developing/Working with Persons with this Behavior.

Realize that a purely intellectual explanation to **Relaters** will not be enough. Their food is the romantic emotional peak or rush of the group interaction. Arguments based on reason only do not work with a **Relater**. Physical separation from people on the job, in the form of work cubicles, is a form of enforced isolation for the Relater. The quiet treatment is sheer torture. The heart has its reasons for which the mind knows not.

- Today, when the opportunity presents itself, say something nice about another person in front of others. Smile at a co-worker or a clerk. Watch his or her reaction. Remember, when you do either of these actions, it may be the only connection that person feels in a day.

Do You Have This Behavior? How to Use It to Your Advantage.

Because there is not a romantic burst of emotional response to you, does not mean that people do not notice or care about you. Bring up that **Builder** and **Planner** part of you. Recognize **Builders** and **Planners** care in a different way. Use your sensitivity to speak their language.

- What are some ways you can indicate caring without a burst of emotional response? List several on the lines below:

_____
_____
_____
_____

My Career Connection: I will seek a job where teams are an integral part of the business.

Your Personal Empowerment Statement: When I choose, I am honest and open.

Color Us Together

Everyone Loves "Snoopy!"

If you are going on any vacation or planning a party, make sure to include a person with strong **Relater** behaviors. **Relaters** love friendly company and amusement. They will always keep the party and conversation going. They are the catalysts of togetherness! They have a sparkling cheerfulness about them. Read the comic strip "Peanuts" and examine the character of the dog, Snoopy, a model **Relater**. (Lucy is the **Builder** and Charlie Brown, the **Planner**.) Basically, **Relaters** wish to enjoy life and to bring the atmosphere of enjoyment to a group. Many are capable of getting overly serious people to look at the lighter side of life. They help others to move away from a morbid mentality of doom and gloom. They are the doom and gloom busters. However, if they have a negative attitude, they may bring strong, emotional pessimism into a relationship. In this mode, they can become very sarcastic. They can turn the art of gossip into a blood bath.

- Collect Snoopy or Ziggy **Relater** cartoons. Even Garfield has moments as a **Relater**. Share them anonymously as acts of kindness or slip them in your own journal or in your son or daughter's notebook. Purchase <u>14,000 Things to be Happy About</u> by Barbara Ann Kippen. Each day select a page at random and read it. Use it as an ongoing energizer for yourself.

Strategy for Developing/Working with Persons with this Behavior.

If you are not a **Relater**, have you ever felt uncomfortable in a group because you didn't know how to keep the conversation going? Were you at a loss for words when voids occurred? Have you wanted to begin a conversation with a stranger but just did not know where to begin? **(Planner)**. Perhaps you have been able to speak out in the past but have lacked diplomacy at times **(Builder)**. Maybe it has been easy for you to speak up, but found people had difficulty in taking you seriously **(Adventurer)**. If any of these descriptions apply, go into training with a **Relater**!

If you or group members are overly serious **(Planners)**, the **Relaters** will help you to smile at yourself. The strength of a **Relater** can create a more open atmosphere for goal attainment.

- Spend some quality time with a **Relater**. Your goal is to understand what motivates he or she. Ask about goals, interests, what is important, what provides fulfillment, etc.

Do You Have This Behavior? How to Use It to Your Advantage.

- Be aware that your gift to bring joy and togetherness is a touch of gold. Learn the **Builder, Planner,** and **Adventurer** languages so you can work more successfully in the contexts they understand.

- What are some situations that might benefit from the team togetherness of the **Relater**?

  _____
  _____
  _____

- Select one of the above situations. What plan of action might be taken in order to improve the spirit?

  _____
  _____
  _____
  _____
  _____
  _____

- Practice being silent when a person is speaking. Silence has a purpose. It is not always necessary to fill the void.

My Career Connection: On the job, in my career, I will take pride in my ability to help people make connections.

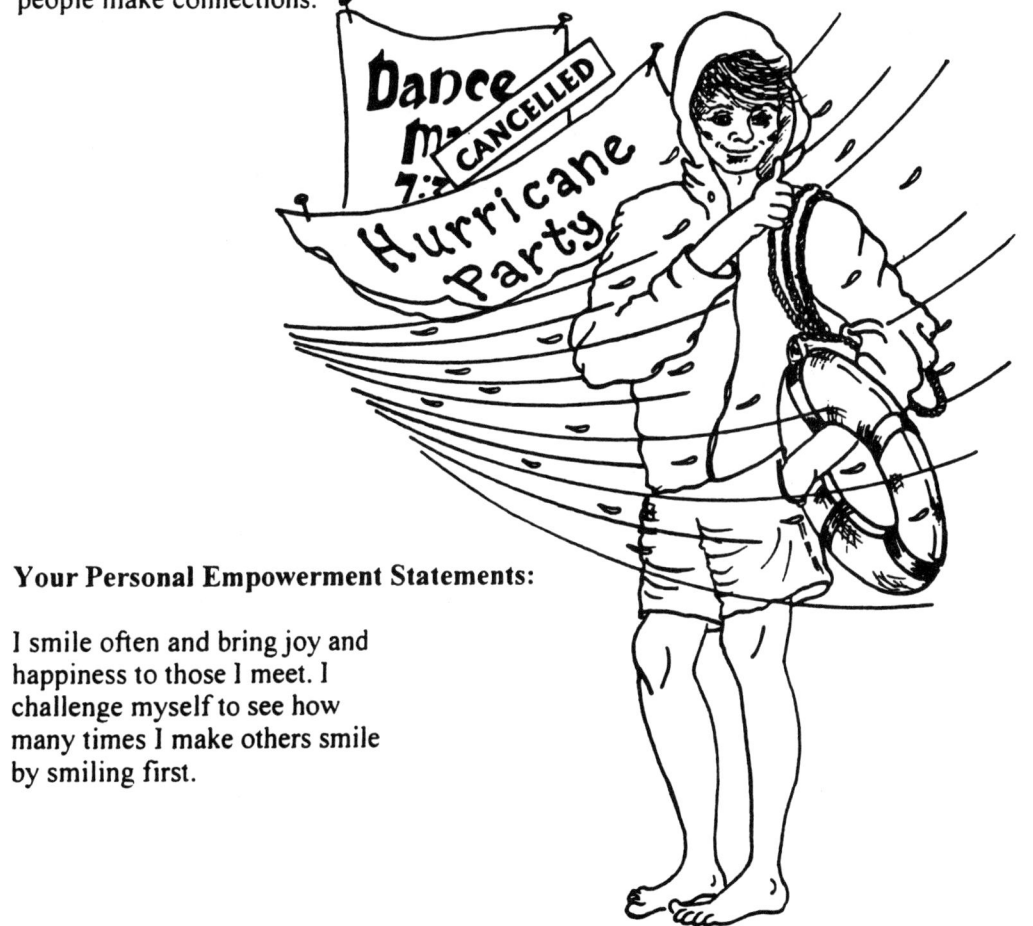

Your Personal Empowerment Statements:

I smile often and bring joy and happiness to those I meet. I challenge myself to see how many times I make others smile by smiling first.

Color Me Wanting Variety

Bees and Flowers

Relater's senses are extremely active when people are around. One impression quickly follows another. **Relaters** are constantly changing moods. There is a certain instability in completing projects.

In contrast to a **Builder** who will respond directly when annoyed, a **Relater** will likely have an emotional outburst. A mother or father with predominate **Relater** behaviors will speak to a delinquent son or daughter in an emotional burst of anger. A little while later, all will be forgiven and she/he will be calm and wonder where the target of her or his anger went? Children often speak of such parents as coming on like the "wrath of God" but after getting the anger off their chests, they revert to gentle lambs. This burst of anger may be carried over to the work world. This is particularly noticeable when **Relaters** are given positions of authority.

Relaters' resolutions are sincere when made, but many times they are not carried out. Their ability to carry through is based on how long their fascination with a task lasts and the length of time and effort required to accomplish it. At home, have you ever agreed to clean up the yard or the garage or to pay the bills, sincerely intending to do so and then been distracted along the way? Did you then deny your lack of consistency, providing an avalanche of valid reasons for why you didn't complete the agreed upon task? This inconsistency runs through the **Relater's** work, entertainment and family life. Relaters love variety in everything. They are like a bee that flits from flower to flower, taking a little nectar here and a little there, but never draining the flower of its potential.

- What are the advantages and disadvantages of changing moods? When emotions change, what is the best way of dealing with the change?

- An excellent resource for studying the **Relater** and an ongoing self energizer is <u>Hope for the Flowers</u> by Trina Paulus.

Strategy for Developing/Working with Persons with this Behavior.

Check out the **Relaters'** sincere promises, especially if they relate to important things in your life. Promises are honestly and sincerely made. Their sincerity makes them more believable because of their powerful emotions. Test and determine if the **Relaters** have gained control over the inconsistency aspect of their behaviors. Examine Relaters' follow throughs in spite of length of time or possible boredom in situations. Any corrections of **Relaters**, if legitimate, will not be held against you.

- Make a list of some positive and negative emotions. Are tears suppressed anger? An emotional release?

Positive emotions	Negative emotions

Do You Have This Behavior? How to Use It to Your Advantage.

Complete all tasks you agree to do. Take into consideration your limitations. Keep your promises to the letter or don't make them. Make changing your word an exception. In general, you should keep your word for credibility, authority and leadership. Write your position out on paper. It will then be a powerful commitment.

- Identify a position you want/intend to take. Write out your position. Stick to your position until you have accomplished it, e.g., speak to one person you have been hesitant to meet or organize something in your personal life. When you have completed your task, return to this page and fill in the date. It is a sign of your success.

_____
_____
_____
_____

Date of completion _____

My Career Connection: I will select a job that contains variety.

Your Personal Empowerment Statement: I derive joy from and have a strong sense of pride in keeping promises. I only make promises I intend to keep.

Color Me Telling It the Way It Is

An Open Book

You will have no difficulty in getting to know the inner lives of those with predominate **Relater** behaviors. They will be open books because they relish talking about themselves and others. Your business is their business! There is no cool reserve as with **Builders** or **Planners**. In fact, many times they say too much, too quickly and live to regret it. Even if this happens, however, they will not grieve long because new fields will have caught their fancy. Secrets are not for them. All you have to do is watch such shows as Jerry Springer, Liza and Jessie Raphael to observe this weakness in action. More than one well-known person, who shared a confidence with a friend, has found that confidence revealed in a tabloid or book. Monica Lewinsky shared with Linda Tripp and an entire country paid the price. Princess Diana learned through painful experience to keep her inner circle small and filled only with discreet friends.

- What is your criteria for sharing inner thoughts with others? Create a checklist.

My Criteria for Sharing:

1. _____
2. _____
3. _____
4. _____
5. _____

Strategy for Developing/Working with Persons with this Behavior.

It is easy to get to know the difficulties of **Relaters**. You will need to be quite stern in establishing limits and holding to them for a productive relationship. Choose your **Relater** friends thoughtfully. All that you say may become common knowledge. They are excellent advisors about the emotional climate around you. You may well avoid strikes and dissension with their helpful input.

- What do you consider a productive relationship?

_____
_____
_____
_____

- Should a person's sex life be talked about in public? What about public figures like the former Princess Diana or the President of the USA?

_____
_____
_____
_____

Do You Have This Behavior? How to Use It to Your Advantage.

Your capacity to elicit and to express your thoughts and inner emotions is quite beneficial. Take care that the person to whom you express yourself is trustworthy. Take the case of a female employee going through a difficult divorce. She poured her heart out to her **Relater** friend prior to taking several days of personal leave. The **Relater** in turn shared with another co-worker who in the utmost confidence shared it and . . . round and round the office went the information. Upon returning to class, the divorcee discovered her privacy had been violated.

- When do you believe it would be dangerous to express one's true feelings and thoughts?

_____
_____
_____
_____

My career Connection: On the job I will use discretion when sharing anything personal about others or myself.

Your Personal Empowerment Statement: I keep secrets entrusted to me like a tomb.

Choose wisely when you choose to tell it all!

- Is this a real secret?
- Does not telling anyone include John and Amy?
- Is this a little secret or a big secret?

Color Me Talking

Your Oprah Winfrey Talk Show Host

Those with strong **Relater** behaviors quickly meet new acquaintances. They associate easily with strangers. Within minutes they are strangers no longer. **Relaters** may keep the atmosphere light and enjoyable in the work environment and at social gatherings.

The role they play in groups depends upon their self-image. If it is negative, they have a great facility for making sarcastic remarks and making people feel badly. Some may be quite obnoxious and dominate the conversation. If the **Relaters** have positive self-images, their delightful humor will enhance productivity and communication.

- Tape an Oprah Winfrey show and a Jay Leno show and compare them. Consider why Oprah Winfrey is viewed as an outstanding example as a talk show host. (She calls on her four parts of self: **Planner, Builder, Relater** and **Builder**).

- Compare the warmth and fun loving style of Howie Mandel to David Letterman or Jerry Springer.

- Consider calumny and detraction. Is it okay for talk show hosts to use trickery and slander as a source of humor? Do they? Why do talk show hosts who use trickery and defamation have a following? Which cluster of behaviors is most likely to make up this following?

_____
_____
_____
_____
_____

- Have you ever been the target of malicious slander? How did you feel?

_____
_____
_____
_____

Strategy for Developing/Working with Persons with this Behavior.

Put **Relaters** in charge of meeting clients or introducing people. They are natural public relation people. You will often find them in sales or people jobs. If they are positive, you can be sure that they will maintain a progressive atmosphere in a group. It is often wise to send a **Relater** to break tragic news concerning death or other misfortunes to another. They will do it in a warm, sympathetic manner that avoids the pitfalls of hopelessness.

- Introduce yourself to the person you least know in your work place or service group. What were the reactions to your overtures? Surprise? Uneasiness? How did you feel?

_____
_____
_____

Do You Have This Behavior? How to Use It to Your Advantage.

If you control your tendency to be frivolous, you will bring a positive healthy atmosphere to any group.

- List rules of thumb for a **Relater** establishing a healthy group atmosphere, e.g., make sure everyone knows the names and has been introduced to everyone.

_____
_____
_____
_____
_____
_____

My Career Connection: I will seek a job where warmth, caring and open communication is valued.

Your Personal Empowerment Statements:
I intentionally say hello and smile at one stranger each day.
I always feel great when I say thank you for the call at the end of a phone conversation.

Color Me Teachable

Seduction

Relaters are very easy to teach when their concentration is maintained. They are not obstinate in holding onto their own ideas, and they receive new information more readily than others do. In the company of incorruptible, progressive people, **Relaters** will flourish and grow quickly. They are pliable and teachable. Good role models are crucial to their growth.

Because of their openness, they may be prime targets for seduction. Their need for other people and the desire to please may override good sense.

- Are there any peer pressure demands locally in your community with regard to young children or teenagers? What are they? The movie <u>Footloose</u> examined this issue.

  _____
  _____
  _____

- If you have children, are there any peer pressures with regard to clothing in your local school or other schools in the area? Groups? Cliques? Gangs?

  _____
  _____
  _____
  _____

- Are there peer pressures on the job?

  _____
  _____

- How does the advertising world enter into controlling what we wear? What we eat? What we buy? How we spend our money?

  _____
  _____
  _____
  _____

Strategy for Developing/Working with Persons with this Behavior.

It is important to control the atmosphere around Relaters. They follow the group. **Relaters** are quite willing to follow the group mentality, be it drugs, cliques or religious cults. They are very open to peer pressure. This is equally true in work situations.

- Can you think of any specific examples where the advertising community has targeted teenagers by creating peer pressure for financial gain?

_____
_____
_____
_____

- How would you evaluate the anti-drug ads on television? Are there any that are effective? Are there any that totally miss the mark?

_____
_____
_____
_____

Do You Have This Behavior? How to Use It to Your Advantage.

Reflect on a group in which you are accepted. Is your tendency to be naive, at times, and easily drawn into situations, perhaps not of your choosing?

_____
_____
_____
_____
_____

My Career Connection: I will hold a job that allows me to work in an atmosphere where we can learn together.

Your Personal Empowerment Statement: I have a wonderful sense of fulfillment as I open my mind up to new ideas and ways of doing things.

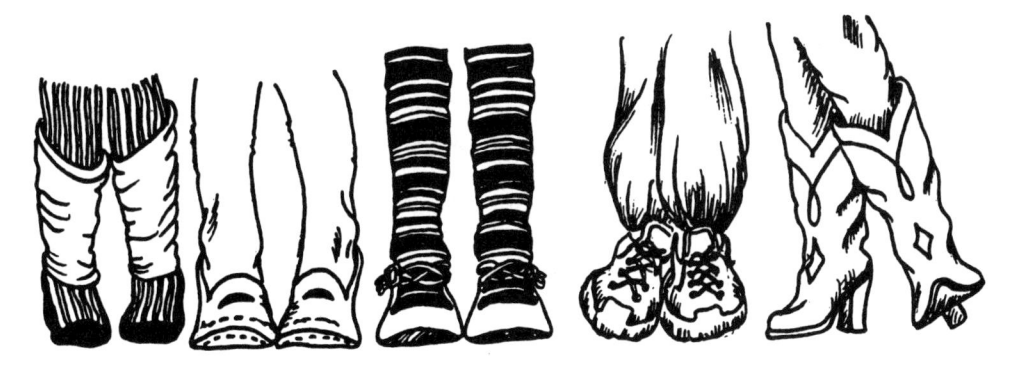

Color Me Praising

Vanity of Vanities

If there is any weakness in the **Relater** part of us, it is that of self-complacency or vanity. This compares to the **Builders** who have not achieved balance, have misplaced ambition and are hard headed; the unbalanced **Planner's** terror of humiliation or the narcissism of the negative **Adventurer**. **Relaters**, if they have not found balance, take childish ecstasy in exterior appearance. When they walk by store windows, they check out their reflections. Your Christmas problems are solved - just purchase mirrors. May you be spared the fate of having three or four **Relaters** in the same house and only one bathroom. They relish flattery, whether giving or receiving it. Praise will reap benefits.

- How do you feel when you are the recipient of false flattery? Why do you think anyone gives out false flattery?

_____
_____

Strategy for Developing/Working with Persons with this Behavior.

Be aware of the **Relaters'** need for praise. Always genuinely congratulate them on a job well done if you want to maintain a productive, future working relationship. Be careful that their praise of you is genuine. Sometimes, it might be mere manipulation to get what they want.

- Give yourself a legitimate compliment for a positive quality you recognize within yourself. Write it on the line below.

_____

Do You Have This Behavior? How to Use It to Your Advantage.

Sincere praise is excellent. Make certain it is based on the action. Haim G. Ginott addresses the importance of appropriate praise for the specific action in his book <u>Between Parent and Child</u>. Examine aspects of your commitments and be certain that you can fulfill the expectations of others. Beauty is more than skin deep; it comes from within the person. You will bring joy to others when you learn to follow through on your promises. You will want to read the "Legend of Narcissus and Echo" often. Narcissus and Echo were exceptionally beautiful and desperately in love with each other. However, when Narcissus caught a glimpse of his beauty in a pool of water, he became fascinated by it. He never looked up again. He was damned to eternal separation and isolation.

- Research the "Legend of Echo and Narcissus." You may obtain a copy of the record/tape of the "Legend of Echo and Narcissus" distributed by Aeon Communications, P.O. Box 7276, Seattle, WA 98133.

My Career Connection: In any job I hold, I will check out the legitimacy of praise I receive or give.

Your Personal Empowerment Statement: I take pride in giving due praise to those about me such as (name or situation).

Color Me Sensitive

The Kangaroo Court

Relaters make excellent, sensitive leaders. The one danger is their tendency to form cliques or favorites. Those with predominate **Builder** behaviors will lead, oblivious to the feelings of others, to the top of the mountain. In contrast, **Relaters** will probably be so concerned about others that they may never get to the top. For **Relaters** it is the enjoyment of people making the journey that is significant, not the goal. In a small clique, they may be the objects of concern. Their need for friendship may lead to being partial and unjust to others whose behavioral styles differ from their own.

- What is your position regarding cloning based on your personal value system?
  _____
  _____

- Refer to the text of In Search of Excellence: Lessons from America's Best Run Companies by Robert Waterman. William A. Andres, former Chairman of the Board of Dayton Hudson Corporation, describes the Hallmarks for Selecting the Best Company in Leadership, Team Building, Self-esteem, Conflict Resolution and Communication manual by Stefan Neilson and Shay Thoelke. He describes cloning in the business world.

Strategy for Developing/Working with Persons with this Behavior.

Put **Relaters** in power who have control over their need for peace and harmony at any cost. If you do not put them in charge, the group may dissolve into several in-fighting parts. **Relaters** love emotional experiences. If they have strong self-images, they will create a positive climate. If they have poor self-images, they may encourage others to fight so they may share in an emotional gratification. They will constantly supply the group with enough conflict to keep it living in hostility for years. You may recall committees, clubs, or church groups, which ended up in a conflict of personalities fanned by the leadership of the **Relater**.

- What happens to a group when there is a person in the group who fans negative emotions, e.g., sows distrust?
  _____
  _____

- Read Games People Play: The Psychology of Human Relationships by Eric Berne, M.D.

Do You Have This Behavior? How to Use It to Your Advantage.

This is a tough one for you. The best guideline would be to seek counsel with a **Planner** or **Builder** as to the merits of those you wish to advance in position or otherwise reward.

- What is the personality make up of the local clubs, gangs or groups in your school or community?
_____
_____

My Career Connection: On the job I will be sensitive to the feelings of my fellow workers and work to achieve harmony in my work place.

Your Personal Empowerment Statement: I am very sensitive to the needs of others such as (name or situation) by giving them a listening ear.

Stirring Up the Pot

Color Me Affectionate

Lady Godiva

Learn to distinguish between the **Relaters'** authentic love and friendliness. They relish emotional encounters. Sometimes, the emotional interaction is more important to them than the person with whom they are relating. For this reason, they love encounter groups and other self-growth seminars. In this atmosphere, they feel emotionally authentic.

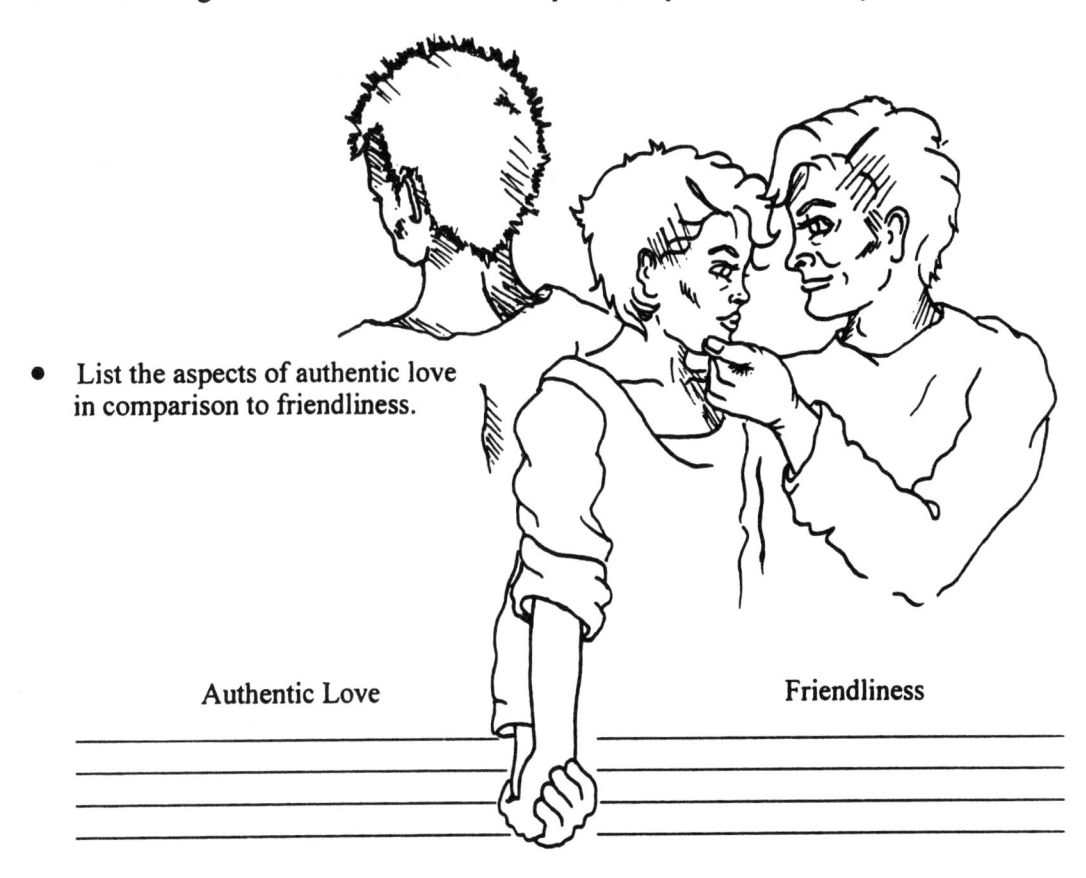

- List the aspects of authentic love in comparison to friendliness.

Authentic Love	Friendliness

Strategy for Developing/Working with Persons with this Behavior.

Check out whether the **Relater** is flirting or serious. Usually time is the best guarantee. Because the American culture basically does not allow exterior signs of caring, as do the Italians, one needs to take this into consideration in any group. Consider a group that was organized for communication growth. There were about forty **Relaters** who consistently attended, displaying affection with hugs and physical touch. Unfortunately, one of the goals of this organization was to attract people from the corporate market. Many top management people are either **Builders** or **Planners**. The group defeated its own purpose by not knowing the language of **Builder** and **Planner** managers and CEOs. When **Builders** and **Planners** attended, the **Relaters**, rather than taking a slow approach, bowled over their guests. Most **Builders** and **Planners**, uncomfortable in such an atmosphere, did not return.

- Have you ever been deceived by what you thought was more than friendliness? One example of this would be sexual harassment. How did you handle it?

_____
_____
_____
_____
_____
_____
_____

Do You Have This Behavior? How to Use It to Your Advantage.

Your friendliness gives life to whomever you meet. Make sure you are giving the right signals of friendliness and not that of implied intimacy. Study the other behavioral trends. A hug to a **Planner** or **Builder** usually implies more than just a handshake.

- What does it mean to be a friend? Does it mean allowing a person to be himself or herself? Can you love a person who is angry or does she/he have to wear a mask?

_____
_____
_____

My Career Connection: I will seek a job where my Relater skills are valued.

Your Personal Empowerment Statement: I am friendly when I choose and authentic when I choose.

Color Me Curious

The Latest News

Relaters like to become involved and know everything that is happening. They have a strong desire to satisfy their curiosity. Their attention is directed to the external rather than to inner logic.

They have a keen interest in their own appearance and that of others. They relish a beautiful body, face, modern clothes, and good manners. They will immediately flick the speck of dandruff off your shoulder. One might say **Relaters** see everything, hear everything, and talk about everything. They have a flow of words that can keep a conversation going for hours. Others may find them too verbose. All of us have met the salespeople that are so busy talking, they don't realize they have already made the sale.

Relaters have an excellent eye for detail, which is an extremely advantageous quality. Whether it be the clothes you wear, the room or office you wish to decorate or the details of an advertising layout, they usually have an eye for what's most suitable.

- Of what value would the **Relater's** eye for detail be in a client presentation, a community project or a new consumer product?

- What courses would be helpful in developing this skill (People Watcher's List)?

- Examine the popularity of sit-com shows. Who do you think are their most avid viewers? Why?

Strategy for Developing/Working with Persons with this Behavior.

Any judgment requiring sensitivity to exterior detail should involve **Relaters**. This detail may involve anything from personal dress to office/home decor. **Relaters** are a must for any social gathering to be an entertaining, enjoyable success.

Watch what you say to **Relaters** unless you want it broadcast. Want a successful office fund raiser in a hurry? Select **Relaters** to be your Paul Reveres. **Relaters** communicate information better than any memos and they do it on a personal level! Wallets and purses will assume the open position.

Until the end of the 1940s, many communities had a party line telephone. This meant multiple homes shared the same phone line. Everyone knew when the telephone operator was listening as there was a familiar click. At the end of a conversation, many would say good-bye to the operator, as a matter of habit. She always responded and they knew that everything, important or trivial, would be communicated by the grapevine.

Do You Have This Behavior? How to Use It to Your Advantage.

Welcome a **Planner** into your confidence. Ask he or she to evaluate your conversational skills and appropriateness of content.

- Why in your opinion do people gossip?
  _____
  _____
  _____
  _____

- Why in your opinion do some people have such a difficult time keeping confidences?
  _____
  _____
  _____
  _____

- Think about the public acceptance and huge circulation of such pulps as The National Inquirer and The Star. Do you find this form of gossip acceptable? Even those who view tabloids as intellectually unacceptable, purchase them anyway. Why? Why would the **Relater** be the main purchaser of such magazines?
  _____
  _____
  _____

- Many of these same buyers are appalled by the behavior of the Paparazzi and yet with their purchases financially support their actions. Why such a double standard?
  _____
  _____

My Career Connection: I will seek to learn something new everyday in my professional life.

Your Personal Empowerment Statement: I deeply respect (person's name or situation) privacy.

The Adult Relater in Summary

Beginning as a child, relating was a motivating force in your life. You were the child who took in the ear torn, battle scarred tom cat. And even when he hissed at your overtures of friendship, you persisted until he finally trusted you. "Lost" dogs followed you home on a consistent basis. You practiced the role of being a caring funeral director as you prepared birds who had flown into windows or fallen out of nests for shoebox burials, flowers included. You were the kid who volunteered to keep the class hamster or rabbit over the summer.

You knew all the characters in Aladdin and the Lion King. When your parents read a Dr. Seuss book to you, they felt like they were an echo chamber. Your friends in trouble found you had a sympathetic ear. If they needed a temporary shelter you were the first to offer your home.

Your room was a personalized statement. The walls of your room were peppered with nail holes as you covered them with multiple changing posters and pictures. Your drawers and shelves overflowed with special treasures that had to be kept forever, including your blanket. Your musical tastes were always changing. Furniture in your room was being continually moved.

Even when you were little you were aware of what was "In" clothing wise. As soon as you could, you convinced your parents of the importance of image statements. Out with Sears "Toughskins" and Penny's mix and match, and in with cool name brands.

Like the kids in *Family Circus*, there was no such thing as a direct route home. Everything was a distraction; friends, neighbors, fire engines, kites caught in trees, anything moving on four legs. You could eat a bowl of cereal, talk on the phone and do your homework at the same time. If you came from a loving family it was your intention to grow up and keep your room at home forever. Your friends were your treasures.

As you grew and moved through the grades your hormones began to rage and you started the process of refining your relating skills. You viewed middle school as a training ground for high school. P.E. shorts were ugly. Faking showers became an art form. All notes had to be folded like Japanese origami paper art. You could write pages and pages about absolutely nothing and pass it to a friend in the morning. By the afternoon you would receive pages and pages of nothing back. But if there was anything private contained in one of these epistles, it was assured of being intercepted. Entrusting a fellow **Relater** with a secret was on a par with putting it up on a billboard. Groups suddenly became all important. Being "In" became a driving force. Getting into an "R" rated movie was a must. Anything censored was like a flame to a moth. If a friend was doing it, it must be okay. This attitude caused you grief on some occasions. You joined multiple musical CD clubs taking advantage of their free disk offerings. Each time it was your sincere intention to return all offerings after you had fulfilled your contract. But, a check of the backseat of your car or under your bed and the odds were you would find unopened CD's you had meant to return. Collection agencies thrived based on your good intentions. You loved giving gifts and if a credit card had been available for paying off other credit cards, you would have applied. Slumber parties and gossip became a girl thing while guys did their thing by just standing around in groups.

High school for you was a multiple of experiences. Through it all, relating continued to be a driving force in your life. The telephone was an extension of you. You could talk for hours. The inventor of the cell phone had you in mind. Your friends continued to be important to you. Sometimes, your friendships could be draining, especially if a friend was having problems. It was difficult for you to put your own needs first and say, "No." You suffered from the "Disease to Please." More than once, hours on the phone helping a friend meant working late into the night to complete your homework or prepare for a test. On the other side of the coin, given a distraction from the drudgery of school work, you would jump the fence at the first opportunity. Staying on task and doing repetitive work was and continues to be a challenge for you.

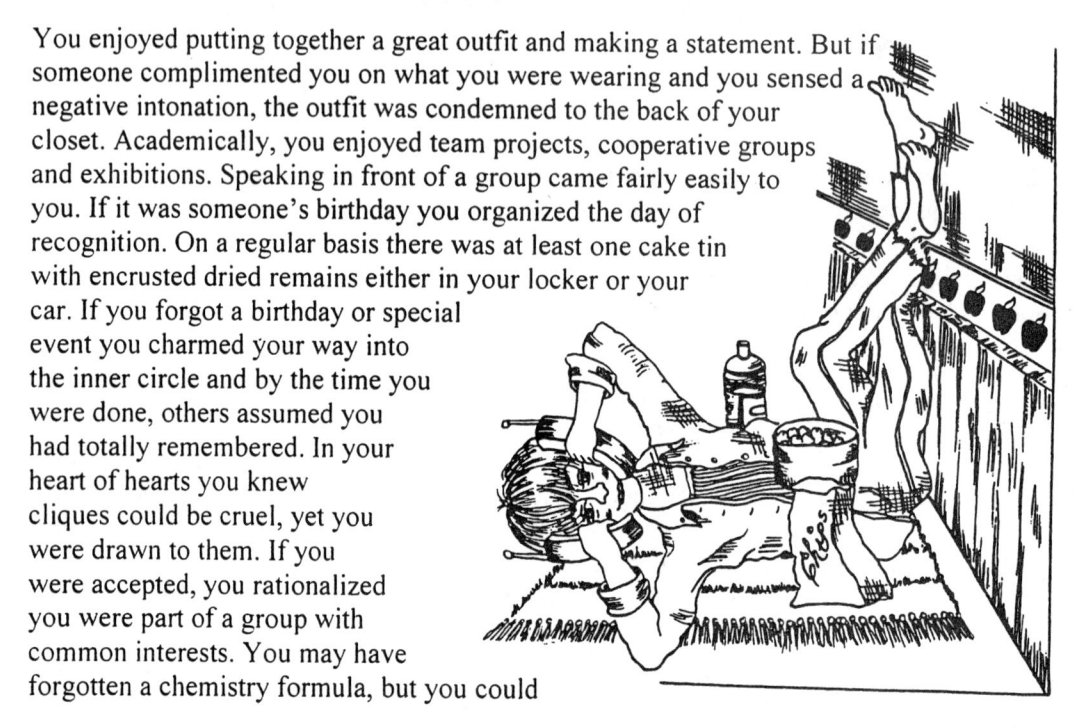

You enjoyed putting together a great outfit and making a statement. But if someone complimented you on what you were wearing and you sensed a negative intonation, the outfit was condemned to the back of your closet. Academically, you enjoyed team projects, cooperative groups and exhibitions. Speaking in front of a group came fairly easily to you. If it was someone's birthday you organized the day of recognition. On a regular basis there was at least one cake tin with encrusted dried remains either in your locker or your car. If you forgot a birthday or special event you charmed your way into the inner circle and by the time you were done, others assumed you had totally remembered. In your heart of hearts you knew cliques could be cruel, yet you were drawn to them. If you were accepted, you rationalized you were part of a group with common interests. You may have forgotten a chemistry formula, but you could describe the complete wardrobes of friends. Large group gatherings were great. You perceived them as wonderful social networks. Then as today, it may be a challenge for your date or spouse to find you before the end of the evening. If your date or spouse is upset, it makes no sense to you. It is a social get together and you were just being "social" and networking.

You love to take pictures. You want people in your pictures. Heads on those people are not necessary. You have shoeboxes and drawers full of pictures. It is your intention to organize and put them into albums. The challenge is to do so before your friends are grandparents.

You are drawn to causes. A fellow worker facing major surgery lacks insurance coverage. A family is burned out of their home. The shelter for the homeless is short on food and supplies. You will be front and center rallying others to join and help correct the situation. Whatever cause you opt to support will be in good hands. Of the four colors you are the most skillful at networking. You could talk Simon Legree and Midas into making a joint donation. Not only will you win them over to make a contribution but you'll also convince them they feel good doing it. Foundations and non-profit organizations will wisely hire you. Nurture your ability to relate.

RELATERS you focus on people. It is this quality that makes you an excellent counselor, nurse, pediatrician, general practice/family physician, psychiatric aide, geriatrics specialist, therapist, assisted living services professional, grief/loss or rape counselor. Your ability to communicate your care and concern can serve as a bridge for those experiencing loss. Read How to Survive the Loss of a Love by Colgrove, Bloomfield and McWilliams and experience the power of **Relater/Planner** empathizing. In little over a hundred pages lacing information with warmth, wit and poetry, they deal effectively and helpfully with the subject of loss. Merv Griffin said, "One of the loveliest books ever written . . . It should be in everybody's library." It is a roadmap for all four colors experiencing loss.

Crooked collars and ties on others draw you like a magnet. You turn neck chains so the clasps are in the back. Lint and threads are to be harvested. You have an eye for exterior detail. You are a wonderful wedding and banquet coordinator. Anything involving presentation is your forte, be it food, stage make-up, costuming, set design, the commercial arts, floral, horticulture, interior decorating, stylist, cosmetics and beauty products, professional photography, product design, boutiques, advertising campaigns, or apparel design. You are the creators of Jamboree® Clothes for Kids and the Gap® for Kids. You are the support team for Tommy Hilfinger and Calvin Klein. You are Gloria Wang designing the perfect wedding gown. You will make the connections between the product and the consumer whether it is Kraft® Macaroni and Cheese, a 4-wheel drive, Estee

Lauder or Eddie Bauer gear. You can take a tract house and turn it into a personalized home with interior decoration. Confronted with a play about cats, you turn it into a memorable event called Cats with your ability to design costumes. Turn the set design over to you and as Maurice Sandak you create an entirely new and timeless The Nutcracker. You are the Anne Geddes of photography as you turn babies into flowered pots, caterpillars and mice. You understand the packaging of any perfume or cologne is as important as the fragrance. Be it crafts, gingerbread houses or wedding cakes, as Martha Stewart, you drive home the importance of presentation and exterior detail.

Although it cannot be proven, in all likelihood it was a **Relater** who established the first support group. They had the wisdom and the experience to recognize that a support group could provide a caring environment for people seeking to change, find solace or to maintain. Take a moment and see how many support groups you can list like Alanon, Widows in Comfort, Weight Watchers and SIDS.

Your motivation is how well you relate with others. You will not be careless or sloppy in relating because you focus on the specific act of relating. As a Relater you will not ignore exterior detail if such disregard would be damaging to a relationship. If personal appearance is a factor in relating, then your choice of tie, shirt and suit will be impeccable. Make-up will be applied meticulously. The birthday floral arrangement you send will contain the recipient's favorite colors. Any gift you give will be personal and the wrapping of the gift will be as important as the gift itself.

You make others feel needed and valued, either intentionally or as a byproduct of your interest. Think about individuals entering into Child Protective Services or the Department of Social and Health Services (DSHS). It is often a demeaning experience. Your ability to make others feel needed and valued serves as the foundation for rebuilding self-esteem, dignity and self worth. The person reporting an insurance loss will find warmth and understanding in your response as an inside telephone insurance adjuster. You take the time to listen. You understand the sense of violation the person is feeling if the loss is due to robbery. Your empathizing skills help you realize the greatest loss in a house fire may be the family photo albums. Your people skills and ability to personalize will serve you well in the professions of insurance agent, broker or hotel concierge.

You thrive in the education profession. Your openness and receptivity to new ideas contribute to your ability to be innovative and creative.

As previously noted nurturing relationships comes naturally to you and carries over to your students.

Children who might otherwise fall through the cracks will find a safety net in you. The classroom with your name on the door will be filled with laughter, fun, warmth and color. It will be a place where young people will feel safe risking in all forms of subject matter. To quote Goethe:

> "Treat people as if they were what they ought to be,
> and you help them become what they are capable of being".

<u>Relationships are of primary importance to you whatever the project or goal.</u> Marriage counseling, family reconciliation and foster care placement are careers where you excel.

<u>Strangers will soon be your friends as a Relater</u>. Every morning as viewers turn their televisions to the *Today* show, Katie, Matt and Al enter our homes like old time friends. We watched Katie Couric in 1990 join the *NBC Today* show as its first international correspondent. In 1991 we saw her become a co-anchor with Bryant Gumble. She has shared with us the birth of her two children. We grieved with her when she lost her husband to cancer in 1998. What is the connection? Her candidness in communicating, her willingness to laugh at herself, her total involvement when interviewing makes us feel like we have known her for years. As a Relater, whether you are communicating one to one or to an audience, you make us feel like we are your focus. Watch Stone Phillips and Jane Pauley in action on *Dateline* as further examples of this talent. Whether the story is about survivors or an investigation concerning product safety, you convey a sense of concern for our well being.

In retail you make us feel valued; that you are truly concerned about helping us make the right choice when purchasing. The size and cost of our purchase is secondary to you. As a manufacturing or pharmaceutical sales representative, your warmth and genuineness will help you to cross the "moat" erected by receptionists. Once you are face-to-face with your client, your friendliness and recall of personal details serve as the basis for a positive and open reception.

You are warm, giving and generous. When you commit to a helping association such as the Chicken Soup Brigade, Housing Hope or UNICEF, you do so with your heart. You are the core of volunteerism. The **Relater** in ministry will have little difficulty building a solid and on-going congregation.

Credit yourself as the Relater in a corporation who can create some sense of a "family" atmosphere. You want harmony in the workplace and will work to achieve it. By your very example, you are a leader in instilling this quality in each of us. You will be the next Carol Bellamy, former director of the Peace Corps and the present head of UNICEF or the founder of the Children's Defense Fund, Marian Wright Edelman. You will make an excellent team player in any group. You will be highly effective in human resources and personnel. You possess the ability to defuse difficult situations. Public relations are one of your strengths. As a receptionist you are the best. You can convince people they do not mind waiting. You are the binding factor in the role of either customer service agent or flight attendant for air passengers.

If you are seeking a **Relater** in the corporate world, check out a company like Saturn. Watch their ads on television. They truly are a reflection of their corporate philosophy. They are people orientated. The ad showing employees painting a fence was taken on site and is real. Yes, their plant is located in the center of a working farm. Their reception area is a renovated historical horse barn. Upon arriving at Saturn to do a presentation, your authors stood out like sore thumbs in business attire. Casual dress was the order of the day. During our actual presentation to a small group of staff, it became evident why Saturn is so successful. They are open and receptive to new ideas and concepts. When we took a break for lunch, it quickly became apparent the warmth we had experienced in our presentation was genuine. We watched as employees wandered in and randomly selected lunch tables. Cliques are not alive and well in this environment, individuals are!

You are the glue of human contact. You are an asset in social work, nursing or the helping associations as a profession. You are willing to reach out to others be they children, the sick, the elderly, the disabled, the homeless or the poor. You helped us with the healing process in Oklahoma City and Littleton, Colorado. You have the ability to make others feel valued and worthwhile regardless of their situations. When you become an advocate you do so on an emotional level. You take the time for the patient who is alone, frightened or confused. Human interaction is vital to your existence.

As a **Relater** your creativity flows. You connect on a personal level and emotional level. Your focus is on all forms of life in this world. You take the time, be it a moment or a day, to see the small things. Consequently, you make wonderful illustrators. Consider the creativity and people connections made by the illustrator Mary Engelbreit. Author Patrick Regan in Mary Engelbreit The Art and the Artist sums up her style: "Cherries, checks, and cottage roses; straw hats, eyeglasses, vibrant colors, quotes and decorative borders--- all are standard elements of a Mary Engelbreit. . . Mary's best illustrations are personal. They are about home, family, and friends--- . . ."

Pick up a copy of LIFE magazine. It's very title speaks to its mission conceived by Henry R. Luce in 1936:

> *"To see life; to see the world; to eyewitness great events;*
> *to watch the faces of the poor and the gestures of the proud;*
> *to see strange things – machines, armies, multitudes,*
> *shadows in the jungle and on the moon;*
> *to see man's work – his paintings, towers and discoveries;*
> *to see things thousands of miles away, hidden behind walls and*
> *within rooms, things dangerous to come to; the women men love*
> *and many children*
> *to see and to take pleasure in seeing;*
> *to see and be amazed;*
> *to see and be instructed..."*

Half a century later its mission statement still stands. Why? Through photo-essays (telling stories in still images) it connects to the **Relater, Planner, Adventurer** and **Builder** in each of us. As a Relater you thrive in this working environment, whether writing copy or taking photographs. Your ability to connect with people is a plus. Your eye for exterior detail sees the third world child standing in the shadow of a doorway. Your creativity provides the focal point in your lens.

Read the works of Toni Morrison, recipient of the Pulitzer for Beloved and the Nobel prize for literature. Her ability to relate touches deep chords within us. Her works include The Bluest Eye, Sula, Song of Solomon, and Jazz, the second book in a trilogy beginning with Beloved. Include the works of Wally Lamb, author of She's Come Undone and I Know This Much. Discover how a male author can write so realistically from a female point of view. When being interviewed on Oprah, he shared that growing up with two sisters, his wife and his female students had provided him with the perspective. As a **Relater**, he not only collected exterior detail, he collected an insightful wealth of emotional experiences. Examine the **Relater** concept of community in Hillary Rodham Clinton's It Takes a Village: And Other Lessons Children Teach Us.

The late Jim Henson left us such a marvelous legacy. He took cloth, wood, plastic and fur and created Kermit the Frog, Ernie, Bert, Miss Piggy and Cookie Monster. Out of pounds of feathers dyed yellow emerged Big Bird. Do you remember waiting for the lid on the garbage can to move, for Oscar to make an appearance? Henson's creations became his ambassadors in the world of children's education and entertainment on SESAME STREET and The Muppet Show. He created such shows as Dinosaurs, The Muppet Babies, The Jim Henson Hour and HBO's first original children's program, Fraggle Rock. Only a **Relater** could have convinced us a pink pig could be sexy and fall in love with a skinny green frog. Jim Henson said, "I believe in taking a positive attitude toward the world. My hope is still to leave the world a little bit better than when I got there." He did.

Your focus is on all forms of life in this world. You are the caring veterinarian. You are the saviors, writers and illustrators of the "Charlottes" (Charlotte's Web) of the world. You can put a Cat in the Hat and make us laugh.

Your ability to connect with people is powerful when you enter the performing arts in drama, dance, acting or directing. Be assured the last category of directing is not limited to men. Julie Taymor was one of two women directors to be the first to win the Tony Award for directing in 1998. Taymor not only directed the Disney's musical The Lion King but, in collaboration with Michael Curry, created some of the most creative costumes and puppets to ever grace a Broadway stage. She combined her talents with the spectacular choreography of Garth Fagan. Add to this the music of Elton John and the lyrics of Tim Rice, who also did the lyrics for Beauty & the Beast and Aida and you have a magnificent quartet team of **Relaters** in action. Read up on Jacques d'Amboise and Trisha Brown if dancing is one of your loves. Study the careers of Tom Hanks, Helen Hunt, Terri Garr, Tom Cruise, Goldie Hawn and John Travolta and you will find a vein rich in **Relaters**.

TIME magazine called her one of the most influential people in arts and entertainment in this century. Her **Relater** strengths are phenomenal. As an interviewer she draws the "real" person out. Sharing her love of reading led to the creation of her Book Club. Go to her web site and click on Changing Your Life and you have access to the experts. Need help with health and fitness, just click another category. She established a national **Relater** connection when she created The Angel Network providing housing for families across our nation. Late in 1998 she conceived of the idea of a Kindness Chain. She cries and laughs with us. She probes deep beneath the surface. She is passionate about life. She is passionate about others. She is passionate about instilling in others a sense of efficacy. She is Oprah Winfrey.

You are a collection of all your experiences, past, present and future. As an artist you effectively can put these experiences on canvas. Examine the works of artist P. Buckley Moss who has spent a lifetime recording in pen, ink and water color the Amish and Mennonites in family and community settings. Even though we may have never ridden in a horse drawn sled, picked a basket of fall apples or attended an old fashion quilting bee, Moss' art makes us feel like we have. When we view her Canadian geese standing in the snow underneath barren trees we may just see geese. But, if we can almost hear the silence, experience the serenity and solitude of the surrounding landscape, the artist has made a connection with us. A relationship has been established. She has related to us and we have understood her message.

You are in the best sense a humanitarian. On September 22, 1960, with its first recruited staff of volunteer doctors and nurses, the S.S. Hope sailed for Indonesia. At that time Indonesia had one hospital, no surgical facilities and only two doctors to meet the needs of 250,000 people. Over the next 14 years she would journey to Vietnam, Peru, Ecuador, Nicaragua, Columbia, Ceylon, Tunisia, the Caribbean Islands and Brazil. The Hope team would serve as both caregivers and teachers. Upon their departure the local practitioners could carry on their work. Project Hope today is no longer a single ship but has become a global organization with land-based programs operating in dozens of countries. The founder of Project Hope was Dr. William B. Walsh. Since his founding vision, HOPE has trained nearly 1.4 million health workers from more than 70 countries. Examples of humanitarian efforts can be found in your own backyard. Seek them out. While researching this section we found a wonderful example located in Snohomish County, Washington. It is called Housing Hope, a non-profit organization committed to providing housing for the homeless.

The same time we arrived to tour the home office located in Everett, a yellow school bus drove up in front and collected five small children. When we asked about it, our guide and co-director explained it would make sense when we reached the heart and center of the agency. As we began our tour we learned Housing Hope targets homeless families in addition to single people who are low income and experiencing mental health illness or who are HIV positive. They presently have 150 transitional and permanent housing units in eleven locations. When someone enters their program, he or she goes through a screening process including chemical dependency. Acceptance is based on a candidate's commitment to turning around his or her life.

Once in the program a case manager is assigned who will train the participant in budget, life skills, employment, vocational counseling and parenting. It is unique in that this organization does not duplicate any services already being offered in the community. Instead, the caseworker serves as a coordinator of these services such as chemical dependency and mental health.

Halfway through the tour, we were informed we had reached the physical center of the agency. We were told we would need to be quiet. The director opened a door and we immediately understood what she had meant by the heart of the agency. Brightly decorated walls, toys, books and small school desks surrounded an open kitchen. The decision to make the kitchen open had been done purposefully. It served as a source of warmth, good smells and security. As we moved through the adjoining rooms we found beautiful children, including sleeping babies watched over by loving staff members. We learned it was a therapeutic child care center specifically designed for homeless children. We also learned the number one victim of homelessness in this country is eight years old. These children were the pulse of Housing Hope.

A powerful aspect of this agency is its Self Help Program. It looks at the challenge of finding housing for the homeless as being on a continuum: temporary shelter to transitional to permanent housing. Upon reaching the end of the continuum, low income families can sign up to build their own homes. Does this approach work? To date more than 100 homes have been built in Snohomish. Simone DeBeauvoir could have been describing the humanitarian **Relater** when she said,

> "One's life has value so long as one attributes value
> to the life of others, by means of love, friendship,
> indignation and compassion."

The actions of **Relaters** are emotion based. Other personalities may think of **Relaters** as non-essential. Don't believe it for a moment! You are the catalyst for reminding all of us of the importance of nurturing our humanity.

Both the **Builder** and **Adventurer** may think the **Relater** wastes time considering feelings. When we cease to take into account the importance of feelings, we deny the importance of all that the **Relater** brings to us. However, reflect on a world without care givers and the relevance of **Relaters** is obvious.

Your Communication Key (feelings):

Build a friendly, caring atmosphere with personal interactions

Your secret vocabulary for

- developing **Relater** behaviors

- getting along with persons with strong **Relater** behaviors:

    * friendly * harmony * people-centered * exterior detail *

    * togetherness * group projects * love * being accepted *

    * giving * honest feelings * teamwork * romantic *

RELATER – Blue

Build an atmosphere of friendly, caring personal interactions.

Comfort zone: Supportive, friendly atmosphere; emotions are crucial; people slogans and posters; harmonious home and teamwork; vocal exchanges such as discussion groups; wants people to like him or her; prefers procedures that are people centered and humanistic; importance of friendliness, sharing; makes self accessible to personal as well as work needs of people; bright well colored, coordinated dress.

Demands on people: Share ideas and feelings, enthusiasm, harmony; speak out in meetings and at home; emotional appreciation; emphasis on exterior detail such as how the report looks, how people are dressed; be democratic.

How to build powerful teams, self-esteem, success, maximum productivity in others and reinforce leadership.

* HOT BUTTONS *

When the **Relater (blue) part of self** in a person is very strong, consider what motivates that person and apply it.

- Take a friendly approach to **Relaters'** communication.
- Provide a social atmosphere and occasions for them to interact.
- Respect other **Relaters'** feelings by not imposing your feelings on them.
- Give genuine concern, a smile, a kind word and do not dominate the conversation.
- Allow them time to talk with their friends in forums such as discussion groups.
- Give occasions for emotional outlets and freedom of their personal expression.
- Smile when passing and congratulate them on various occasions especially when they least expect it.
- Control is needed for younger individuals, but do it warmly and lovingly.
- Note how the report looks, how people are dressed - be democratic.

Winning Colors®
Validates who you are
And gives you the tools
To validate others . . .

How I Find Out About The Adventurer Part of Me

Some Observable Behaviors with Exercises for Developing Them

Color Me In Action

Color Me an Adventurer

Let's get this show on the road. The magic word is excitement! "Move it, man, move it!" The following distinction is critical when dealing with an **Adventurer**. Excitement is the key. Things get done because of the excitement involved in the urge or whim of the moment. Sitting is boring. The **Adventurer** part of ourselves has the spirit of the mountain men and frontiersmen. Mountains are to be scaled; and slopes of snow carved. The frontiers of space and the oceans are to be conquered. They are the "Mud Hole" Smith, Eddie "the Eagle" Edwards or "Wop" May and Max Ward - the bush pilots of the wilds of Alaska and far north. They are the female mushers Susan Butcher, Dee Jonrowe and Lolly Medley Wasilla of the Iditarod. They are Jacque Cousteau of the oceans, Robin Williams and Whoopi Goldberg of comedy, Madonna of music, pilots of intrigue and John Glenn, who after traveling to outer space decades ago, returned at the age of 76. They are Eileen Collin, the first woman commander of the Space Shuttle Columbia.

- Make a list of local, positive, exciting, available action. An example would be the REI Rock Climbing Center.

_____   _____
_____

Strategy for Developing/Working with Persons with this Behavior.

As long as the action is exciting, the **Adventurer** is an excellent person for the job. Make sure you have the reins well in hand. Above all, make sure the action is directed toward the end result that you wish to attain. It will be up to you to focus the action.

- Is there a gang mentality in some business concerns?

_____
_____

- Think about pressure groups in terms of action merely for action's sake. How could a pressure group's actions be productive?

_____
_____

Do You Have This Behavior? How to Use It to Your Advantage.

It would be prudent for you to discover where your excitement is leading. The payoff is that you will venture into positive actions that will lead you to both more of the same and to appreciation.

- Can you think of any recent reports in the news of positive and negative actions? A rescue? A stunt?

_____
_____

My Career Connection: I will seek a job that allows me freedom of action.

Your Personal Empowerment Statement: I am an action person getting things done.

Color Me Testing the Limits

Climb the Highest Mountain

Tiredness, hunger and pain are all part of the adventure. Hardship is to be endured. It is the cost of the action and excitement. Discomfort is part and parcel of the glory of climbing Mount Everest. Yet, discomfort was the last thing on the minds of Edmund Hillary and Tenzing Norgay on May 29, 1953 when they were the first to reach the summit of Everest. Kris-Ann Bancroft was the first woman to journey to the North Pole by dogsled and skis. In 1992, she led a group of women to the South Pole. In 2001, she joined Liv Arnesen as the first to ski across Antarctica. The more rugged the sport, the better!

- Why in your opinion do people climb Mount Everest? It costs time, money and lives.
  _____
  _____
  _____

- Read <u>Into Thin Air: A Personal Account of the Mount Everest Disaster</u> by Jon Krakauer to gain insight into the driving forces behind such efforts and the costs.

- Make a list of exciting positive adventures available in your area. Put a star by those adventures you have always wanted to experience.

Strategy for Developing/Working with Persons with this Behavior.

If the action demands endurance, you can be assured that once the **Adventurers** commit themselves, they will reach their goals. Challenges are an integral part of their lives.

- List work that is available for those of an adventurous spirit. Be sure to list the demanded endurance connected with the work, e.g., Jacques Cousteau's explorations, stunt people, firefighters, detectives and astronauts.

- **Adventurer** behavior surrounds us in our daily lives. Can you identify this behavior in someone you know?

_____
_____
_____
_____

Do You Have This Behavior? How to Use It to Your Advantage.

Choose your adventure well and if you seek fame, you will be listed among the great explorers and frontiersmen of history. The jungles, the ocean floors and space await you.

- Have fun and be challenged. Make a historical list of explorers up to the space age and the contributions that they have made.

Career Connection: I will have a career that allows me to test the limits.

Your Personal Empowerment Statement: I enjoy the journey to my goal (name) and take any setback in stride.

Color Me Free

Don't Fence Me In!

"Don't Fence Me In", an old song made famous by Bing Crosby, expresses the basic value of the **Adventurer** - a*bsolute freedom of action.* **Adventurers** are the advocates of a *laissez-faire* world. "Give me land, lots of land under starry skies above. Don't fence me in! Let me ride through the wide-open country that I love. Don't fence me in!"

The **Adventurer** hears the wind as it begins to stir, senses the ripple as it moves across the lake, feels the sensuousness of the black velvet evening sky. Being alone on a glacial lake, standing in the shadows of the Angkor monuments of Cambodia or diving in the silence of the Great Barrier Reef all call out to the **Adventurer.** The **Adventurer** is as comfortable being alone as in a group, provided the group is headed in the same direction he or she has targeted. Some studies involving brain scans suggest that when the **Adventurer** type is not engaged in action, brain activity appears to be on the equivalent of a computer in the sleep mode. This does not mean the senses are in a sleep mode. Rather in the Adventurer the senses are like a radar scope, continually scanning and sweeping the surrounding area for potential action.

The **Adventurer** is interested in the action rather than the goal. The advantage is that tradition or a lifestyle that brings mental death and boredom to many others does not bind the **Adventurer**. The **Builder** may stay at a job because of a sense of duty, the **Relater** because of attachment to people, the **Planner** because of the personal investment but the **Adventurer** will stay if diversity and change are present.

- Can you think of any **Adventurer** songs? List a couple of them below:

  _____
  _____
  _____
  _____

Strategy for Developing/Working with Persons with this Behavior.

Adventurers may be insensitive to the pain caused because of the ease with which they might sever social ties. They may walk away from school, friends, family, job or situations without a backward glance. Responsibilities may be tossed to the winds as quickly as they are assumed. Direct their energy in a positive way, don't block it!

- Can you think of any situations where you experienced pain because an individual in your life walked away from his or her responsibilities?

_____
_____
_____

Do You Have This Behavior? How to Use It to Your Advantage.

It would be profitable for you to seek out the input of a **Relater** when dealing with people. Beware that the action you are involved in might build a "Third Reich!" The *gang* a teen age youth selects may destroy the individual in the end. The same is true for adults.

- How does the **Adventurer** have the advantage over the Relater in Public Speaking or presentations?

_____
_____
_____

My Career Connection: I will seek a job that will not inhibit my sense of free expression.

Your Personal Empowerment Statement: I delight in the thrill of (being with _____ or situation).

Color Me Traveling

Born Under a Wandering Star

Adventurers love to travel. They live on change. They are the natural-born hoboes. The words "Born under a wandering star," sung by Lee Marvin in <u>Paint Your Wagon</u> aptly illustrates this characteristic: "I was born under a wondering star, a wandering, wandering star. Hell is in hello forever, it's time for me to go." When the town became *civilized*, it was time to move on.

- Have you ever wanted to chuck it all and walk away? If you did, how did you feel? If you did not walk away, why and how did you feel?

___

- How does a career in the military meet the **Adventurer's** need for challenge and change?

___

Strategy for Developing/Working with Persons with this Behavior.

Punishment for those with predominate **Adventurer** behaviors is not as effective as with other clusters of behaviors. They will have difficulty understanding why they are being punished. Life should be enjoyed. There will be a natural lack of any kind of commitment or follow-through from them, for they will be on to new fields of action. Usually, **Adventurer** salespersons do not have a natural instinct for following-up after a sale. Their interest is in the challenge of the next sale, the new potential customer. **Planners** and **Relaters** are more interested in maintaining the relationship.

- How would you define the purpose of punishment?

___

- Many times punishment increases negative behavior and thus reinforces it. In your personal life have you either experienced this outcome or observed it? Explain.

___

- Do you think the prison system reinforces negative or positive behavior? If so, how?

___

Do You Have This Behavior? How to Use It to Your Advantage.

Take a good look at your follow-through with people. If you wish trust and faithfulness, it is crucial you show that you are not a whimsical person. Keeping tabs on your old friends as well as your new ones will serve to nurture your relationships.

- What opportunities exist for the Entrepreneur in the business world?

___

- Would the **Adventurer** be able to survive in an Organized Corporation, e.g., the banking system? Why or why not?

___

My Career Connection: I will have a job that does not pin me down emotionally or physically unless I choose to do so.

Your Personal Empowerment Statement: Traveling (name place and persons) and experiencing new things is exhilarating to me.

Color Me Taking Risks And Chances

Master of Spontaneity

Life should be lived on the trapeze. The Flying Wallendas didn't just think life should be lived on a high wire, they lived it. Today Steven Wallenda's advertising motto is:

> **"If it's possible – It's been done.
> If it's impossible – It will be done.**

To be spontaneous is to be alive. The thrill of dynamite exploding, the rush of the air passing by while skydiving should not be dampened by the duty of attachment. Consider the exploits of Indiana Jones in the **Raiders of the Lost Ark**. Epicurus is credited with the philosophy of eat, drink, love, and be merry for tomorrow we die. As a footnote he advocated moderation in all. Few, including the **Adventurer** remember Epicurus' footnote. For those with predominately **Adventurer** behaviors, tomorrow never comes. The soldiers of fortune must find a new cause. If that cause should save a civilization, it is secondary. What counts is the excitement of the journey. It is the ride on the roller coaster that matters, the arrival at the terminal is boring. Many rock stars are **Adventurers**, e.g., Sting. On a more serious note, everyday around the world, men and women in the military put their lives on the line. It may be a Marine standing duty at the American Embassy in Salzburg, a soldier taking his place on the demarcation line in Korea or a fighter pilot scrambling into the cockpit of an F-18 responding to an intruder.

- Good examples of the quick thinking of the **Adventurer-Planner** can be found in such television series as "SG1," " Cops," "Chicago Hope" and "E.R." If you have the time watch one of these shows.

- What would be some examples of risk-taking in a military environment?
  _____
  _____
  _____
  _____

- What do you think is the driving motivation of Red Adair? He is a professional firefighter and was responsible for putting out the oil fires in Kuwait after the Gulf War.
  _____
  _____
  _____
  _____

- How is risk-taking a part of being a salesperson?
  _____
  _____
  _____
  _____

Strategy for Developing/Working with Persons with this Behavior.

You must provide an atmosphere of movement if you wish to keep **Adventurers** faithful. A home or school that runs on graveyard time will alienate **Adventurers**.

- Any project that involves action would keep the attention of the **Adventurer**. The key is to direct her/him in a positive, result-oriented way. Are there any positive action goals in your school, community or on the job?

_____
_____
_____
_____

Do You Have This Behavior? How to Use It to Your Advantage.

Your life's challenge is to respect tradition and the stability that society needs in order to grow and evolve.

- Make a list of traditions that would hassle the **Adventurer**. Would any of those traditions listed be a hassle for you? If you struggle with this question, start with the traditions in your family. The holidays or vacations are good starting points.

_____
_____
_____
_____
_____

My Career Connection: I will consider how important risk is to my motivation in my work.

Your Personal Empowerment Statement: It gives me a rush to undergo exciting experiences safely.

DO IT NOW!

Color Me Celebrating

Merry Christmas, Happy New Year

Adventurers want to see Christmas and New Years continue for 365 days a year. There is no desire to work in the traditional sense of the word. Work should be fun, not drudgery. Playful is their watchword. A cruise ship, a magical Disney Kingdom performer, the circus, testing sports equipment, driving the Oscar Mayer Wiener truck, professional clown or mime, a social director, a safari guide, a cartoonist are just a few of the avenues calling out to the fun loving **Adventurer**.

- Although this behavioral style is unacceptable in the **Builder** school/business system, there is a special challenge in helping the **Adventurer** gain self-esteem. What are some things you or others could do to develop or reinforce an **Adventurer's** sense of self-worth?

_____
_____

- How does a **Builder** perceive the value of the **Adventurer** and visa versa?

_____
_____

Strategy for Developing/Working with Persons with this Behavior.

Your best chance of success when working with **Adventurers** is in a party atmosphere. As long as they are performing in the limelight, the work you want completed will be accomplished. If you are seeking action and results, work with an **Adventurer**.

- Give the **Adventurers** an opportunity to enjoy the limelight legitimately. Set strong limits and hold on to them. List situations where they can work off their pent-up steam according to your situation.

_____

Do You Have This Behavior? How to Use It to Your Advantage.

Check out the task and determine if there is a continual atmosphere which brings out your best. That is why entertainment, professional sports, firefighters, soldier of fortune, astronaut, entrepreneur, or detective, etc. usually offer the best areas for your continued success.

- What are legitimate local outlets for those whose primary strength is **Adventurer**? If you don't know, ask some **Adventurers** to share theirs with you. (Notice we have used the word legitimate, e.g., legitimate race tracks.)

_____
_____

- Are there any local negative outlets for **Adventurers**? If so, what are they?
  _____
  _____

My Career Connection: I must carefully seek a non-traditional work environment.

Your Personal Empowerment Statement: I join in the spirit and action of festive occasions such as (name) with (name).

A very merry un-Christmas
to you
A very merry un-Christmas
to you-to you!

Color Me A Seeker

Chuck Yeager . . . Amelia Earhart . . . Jacques Cousteau

There seems to be a slight contradiction in regard to the behaviors of the **Adventurers**. On the one hand, they love action and excitement; on the other hand, they may be quite leisurely in attitude when there is nothing to amuse them.

A prime example of this is shown in Paint Your Wagon through the character played by Lee Marvin. In many scenes, he is either in the midst of a crisis or creating one. The **Adventurers'** leadership ability to handle a crisis in a cool, adept, practical and successful manner is astounding. Note the manner in which Tom Cruise as the **Adventurer** lawyer dealt with Jack Nicholson the powerful Marine **Builder** in A Few Good Men. Sometimes, however, when the world is crashing down upon everyone else, they go merrily on their way with little concern. Body movements are rather quick when action and excitement are involved. Otherwise, **Adventurers** will take their time and your time! "Manana is soon enough for me!"

However, the more time one spends examining the behaviors of the **Adventurer**, the more it becomes apparent that the media stereotyped this personality extensively. There is a tendency to assume that this personality, in its purest form, is personified in "Indiana Jones."

Turning to the history books, one will find a marvelous list of candidates. Upon reviewing Jack Gorner's The Search for Amelia Earhart one finds a woman of quiet dignity and courage who left everything behind on a secret mission for her country. Someday, when all the President Roosevelt archives are opened, we will be allowed to honor and acknowledge this magnificent **Adventurer**! Consider such names as Chuck Yeager, who left the earth in a Bell-X-1, courtesy of a broom handle. He was the first man to go faster than the speed of sound while all those on the ground maintained it was impossible. Jacques Cousteau, opened up an entire world to us. He allowed the adventurous seed within each of us to dive under the ice cap and to swim side-by-side with the great turtles.

It would be easy to classify the previous names listed as **Adventurers** only, but this would not be true. When one examines Golda Meir, it is apparent that she possessed the balance of a **Planner/Builder/Relater/Adventurer**. According to reports, Meir had sent a team of over 20 men on a raiding mission into the Sinai. After several hours, the team reported they had been exceedingly successful. Then, she learned that one young man had been killed. It is reported that she recalled the mission, saying that the loss of one Israeli was one too many. Her central trend, **Builder**, provided the leadership, her **Planner** behaviors planned the mission, the **Adventurer** in her took the risk, and the **Relater** recalled the mission. Virtue lies in the balance of qualities.

- Be prepared for the **Adventurer** behavior. Understand they will act out the **Adventurer spirit**. Save yourself from ulcers and prepare a plan of action. Channel the energy.

Strategy for Developing/Working with Persons with this Behavior.

If you want the excitement of moving into the unknown, along a path riddled with crises, join ranks with **Adventurers**. **Adventurers** are at their best in a crisis. Life is an adventure to be lived fully each moment. If you are able to survive the action and danger, you will reap the thrill that rushes through the **Adventurer**.

- Many people suffer from the pressure of stress. The ability to relax and "let go" is an admirable quality that may be learned from the **Adventurer**. What are some outlets you could use for releasing stress?

_____
_____
_____
_____
_____

Do You Have This Behavior? How to Use It to Your Advantage.

Study the lives of **Adventurers** like Christopher Columbus, Chuck Yeager, Amelia Earhart, and Jacques Cousteau and see the excitement, action, and honor that is given to them in the history books. If your actions, group, or goals have a positive direction, you may reap every possible thrill and at the same time benefit both yourself and the people around you.

My Career Connection: I will seek a career that allows me to grow and evolve.

Your Personal Empowerment Statement: I am a natural born explorer.

No pessimist ever discovered the secrets of the stars, or sailed to an uncharted land, or opened a new heaven to the human spirit
  -Helen Keller

Color Me Playful
Might Have Gone Fishing

Adventurers have little desire to work in the traditional sense. They dislike the daily routine of the corporate structure, establishment, or the bureaucracy. With no sense of guilt, they leave everything behind that is not of interest. As the old song goes: "Might have gone fishin'. Got to thinkin' it over. The road to the river is a mighty long way. It's my lazy day!" Everything is seen in terms of enjoyment. Without the thrill, all else proceeds and develops slowly. No matter how you try to speed things up, you'll be wasting your effort unless excitement is involved. They respond to their own impulse, not yours.

- Identify three successful entrepreneurs. What were the factors involved in their success?

_____   _____   _____

Involved factors:
_____
_____

- Identify some magazines in which one will find a preponderance of **Adventurer** ads.

_____
_____

- Is there anywhere in your community where creative graffiti could replace scribbles on the walls?

_____
_____

Strategy for Developing/Working with Persons with this Behavior.

Brush up on your patience if you want the support of **Adventurers** in the daily routine of life. McDonald's advertisement of a "Great Time and a Great Taste!" hits at the heart of the **Adventurer** mentality.

- Identify three ads that would appeal to an **Adventurer.** List them below. Assess their impact on all four colors.

Ad # 1
_____

Impact on the other three colors
_____

Ad # 2
_____

Impact on the other three colors
_____

Ad # 3

Impact on the other three colors

Do You Have This Behavior? How to Use It to Your Advantage.

If you wish to be successful in the future in a corporation, it will be necessary that you learn to operate within the sometimes repetitive nature of the work. In general, it would probably be best to seek out action centered companies rather than ones with established traditions. You will probably find a more compatible niche.

My Career Connection: I will examine all potential careers to determine whether I can use my behavioral strength to my advantage.

Your Personal Empowerment Statement: I have a great time and have fun joining in with (name).

*How many cares one loses
when one decides not
to be something
but to be someone*
               -Coco Chanel

Color Me Generous

The Ant and the Grasshopper

In the tale of the ants and the grasshopper, the ants labored all summer to prepare for the winter. The grasshopper played his fiddle and chided the ants for their labor. When winter arrived, the grasshopper was not prepared and would have starved to death in the end without the generosity of the ants. The grasshopper clearly takes on the role of the **Adventurer**, who lives in the present. Yesterday is of no value in memory and tomorrow will take care of itself.

The past and the future are simply pushed aside by the fullness of the present. Of course the **Adventurer** learns from the past. However lessons are applied primarily for the full life of the present. The grasshopper knew very well that winter would come, but passing up the living of today for the working preparation for winter simply didn't make sense since there was fiddling to be enjoyed today. Tomorrow there might be more fiddling or something else, but the "grasshopper" won't worry about it now.

Adventurers are generous with what they have <u>and</u> what you have. There is little distinction. They are masters of the grand gesture. Share and share alike. Your desk materials, your cosmetics, your clothes, your car, your food are all up for grabs.

- There is a fine line between sharing and using people. In your opinion what is the difference?

_____
_____

Strategy for Developing/Working with Persons with this Behavior.

If you are in a close relationship with an **Adventurer**, make sure you specify what money or goods are available. Set specific limits and establish a method of control. Parents or employers may have a son or employee that is quite happy living off what is provided. For example, as long as you provide the essentials, they will feel no guilt for taking your generosity. If you kick them out of the house, they will move into the garage. Kick them out of the garage, they'll move into the back yard. Your strategy: cut out food, water and shelter. Keep in mind that this attitude is not ill will. Their thinking is: "Why should I go through the boredom of making a living or doing boring things when others will do it for me? This gives me the time to do what I want - endless action and excitement!"

- Think about the traditional work ethic; man must work by the sweat of his brow. How is that changing with the modern leisure society? Consider the role of the robot. What are some of the advantages the **Adventurer** would have in the new world?

_____
_____

Do You Have This Behavior? How to Use It to Your Advantage.

Be thankful if you have a strong **Adventurer** presence. It is that part of you that the **Builder** finds irresponsible, the **Planner** finds very shortsighted and the **Relater** finds too individualistic. They all, however, envy your ability to focus so completely on the present. You are not burdened by the lessons and pitfalls of life and give full attention to work and play.

- Think back on your last encounter with a **Red** in your daily life. What was your first impression of the **Adventurer**?

_____
_____

My Career Connection: My **Adventurer** attitude is strength, but I will temper it on the job.

Your Personal Empowerment Statement: Spiritual and material things come to me abundantly and I share my good fortune with others (name or situation).

Color Me An Explorer

The Call of the Wild

Many **Adventurers** respond to the "Call of the Wild!" They are the Susan Butchers of the world. In 1978 she entered her first Iditarod. She finished in the top five every year with the exception of 1985. She holds the record for the fastest record for course completion and is one of only two people to have won the Iditarod four times. No small achievement when one understands the Iditarod trail stretches from Anchorage to Nome Alaska on the western Bering Sea coast. Each team consists of 12 to 16 dogs and a "musher." Their challenge is to cover over 1,150 miles in 10 to 17 days through Arctic wilderness. The temperatures vary from –62 degrees centigrade to 0 degrees centigrade. There is a tendency to assume given such a goal an **Adventurer** will go all out and let nothing get in their way. In one of Susan Butcher's races she was a leading contender when a moose, without warning, came crashing into her team, injuring one of her dogs. She immediately dropped out of the race and returned to get medical treatment for the injured dog. Anyone who has seen her in person or heard her lecture knows she is a humanitarian first and a musher second.

Adventurers are the Evil Knieval personas of the world. They will live in the trees of the rain forest cataloging flora and fauna. They are willing to risk all in finding cures for world diseases.

"They have no strings to hold them down," as Pinnochio sang, "To make me fret, to make me frown. There are no strings on me!" Planning our life in advance takes the fun out of living.

- Think about our educational system. Many youths hold a negative Adventurer attitude regarding the school system. **Adventurers** do not mind the pain, effort and struggle of learning. What bothers them is traditional learning. Sitting in rows and boxes is not for them. Reading a chapter and answering the canned questions at the end of the unit is *borrrring!* Work sheets to **the Adventurer** are on the same level as filling out IRS forms. The formal lecture approach sends them out in space to the farthest corners of the universe seeking relief from the stagnant droning. When caught in such situations the desk he or she is sitting in may become the focus of reconstruction. Bolts and screws will quietly be removed. Frames will be bent. The desktop will be covered with carved etchings. They learn far better building a fort than just reading about it. Why do you think the educational system is so slow in responding to the **Adventurer's** style of learning?

There is a crucial need for more red **Adventurer** teachers in education, yet they are few in number. Why?

_____
_____

Strategy for Developing/Working with Persons with this Behavior.

You will have a real companion when you are involved in the challenge of new worlds - outer space or the unexplored territories. Adventurers have an ability to take on hardships with greater ease than any other does.

Do You Have This Behavior? How to Use It to Your Advantage.

Make sure that your partner in your adventure has the supplies to back you up. You may find yourself in the middle of the Alaskan wilds with no sled, dogs and food. Twenty-four hours of sun will not keep you alive and warm.

My Career Connection: I will have work that allows me to focus on the new, the unknown, the unexplained, the edge, the unexamined, and the never before.

Your Personal Empowerment Statement: When the going gets rough, I get going (with person or situation).

Color me Being Concrete

The Sensual Touch

Adventurers are usually sensual by nature, whether it is the twist of a wrench or a touch of a kiss (James Bond). These have much more meaning and motivation than an avalanche of words. In our seminars, we show videos from the advertising world. We have noticed that many of the jean ads, e.g., Jordach or Wrangler turn off all the participants except the **Adventurer**. The advertising world spends millions to identify their clients. They adapt their ads to the behaviors of the buyer. Accountability and duty are not words for the **Adventurer**. But riding the back of a stallion, floating on the winds in a hot air balloon attempting to circle the world, sky diving or roaring down the track in a race car will trigger the adrenaline of any **Adventurer.** Thrill them, don't appeal to their sense of duty. A.J. Foyt, four time winner (1961, '64, ' 67, '77) qualified for a record 35 consecutive times at the Indianapolis 500. Add the names Emerson Fittipaldi, Mario Andretti, Michael Andretti, Rick Mears, Al Unser, Bobby Unser, Parnelli Jones, Janet Gutherie and you have a starting list of the great **Adventurer** drivers. Accountability will naturally follow as they are at their best in the midst of physical, sensual action.

- How does sensuality differ from sex? A comparison of the Italian to U.S. culture can serve as a starting point.

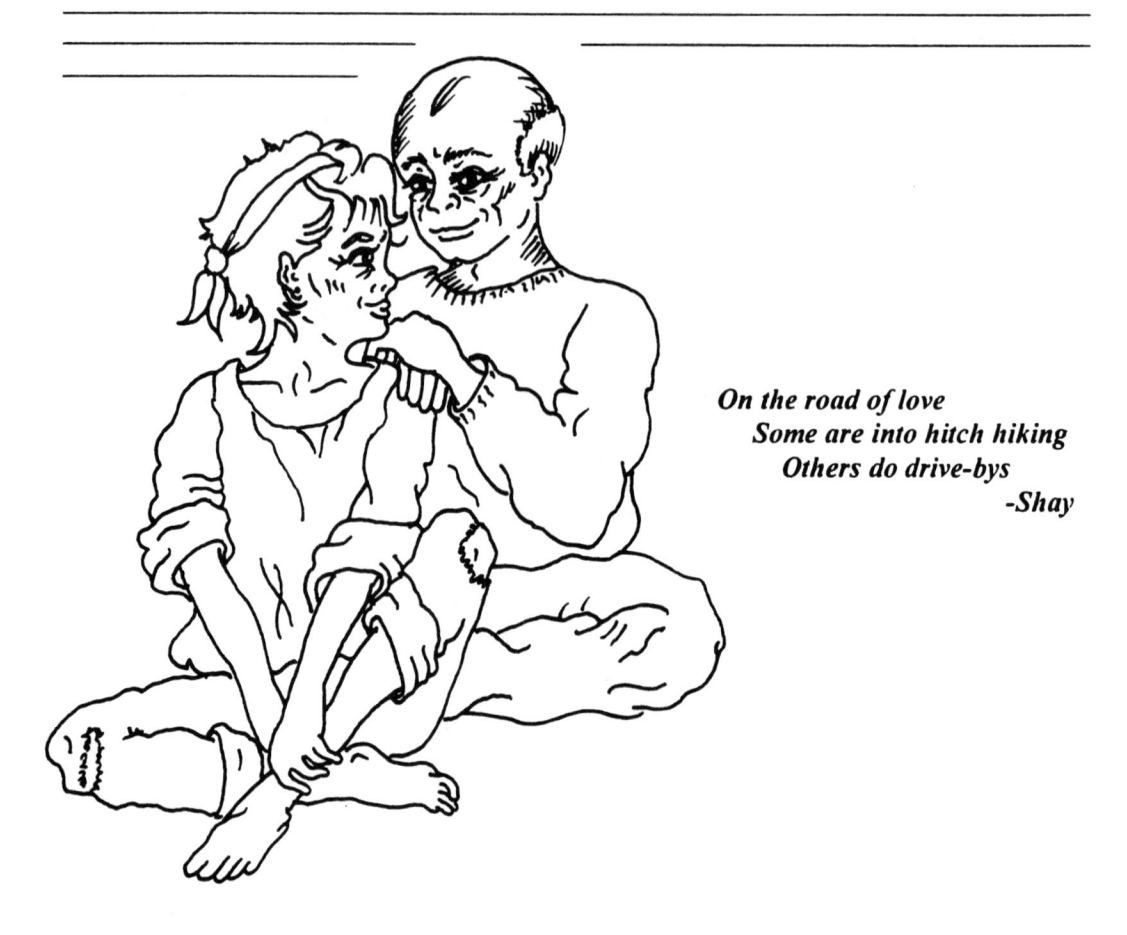

_____   _____
_____

On the road of love
Some are into hitch hiking
Others do drive-bys
-Shay

Strategy for Developing/Working with Persons with this Behavior.

If you have organized, theoretical plans that depend on the **Adventurer** for their success, you are in trouble. If you have concrete action plans that you can feel, touch, and experience, your best bet is a qualified **Adventurer**. Their learning style tends to be tactile.

Do You Have This Behavior? How to Use It to Your Advantage.

Look for opportunities to further develop your action skills. Although you are usually good on the spur of the moment, a little practice will usually rocket you to success. Learning **Builder, Planner**, and **Relater** behaviors will enhance the experience.

- It will be your challenge, when dealing with peers or younger youth, to separate those who would like to be **Adventurers** from those who are **Adventurers**. This will be most helpful for the understanding of self. It is crucial **Builders, Relaters or Planners** realize it is peer pressure and the advertising industry's focus on the Adventurer that often pressures them into disowning their behavioral strengths. Help them to be proud of their **Builder, Planner** and **Relater** behaviors.

My Career Connection: I will focus on being accountable on the job/in my career.

Your Personal Empowerment Statement: My sense of touch gives me new and exciting information.

Color Me Quick to Respond

Mission Impossible

Adventurers are usually whizzes when anything mechanical is involved. Whether it is a jet, rocket, sports car, or bulldozer, the **Adventurers** often have the advantage. The bigger, faster, more exciting or challenging the machine, the more you will whet the Adventurers' appetites. Note films of Jean Claude van Damn, JAG, Chuck Norris or Stephen Seagal films. Consider how the books of Robert Ludlum and Tom Clancy appeal to the **Adventurer** in each of us. Robert Ludlum is the author of 21 novels, published in 32 language and 40 countries. They have worldwide sales in excess of 20 million copies. Conclusion? The appeal of the **Adventurer** knows no boundaries. Tom Clancy is the author of 15 major novels. In his first novel, he took to the sea in <u>The Hunt for Red October</u>. It has since become a classic movie seen by millions. When you are reading one of his novels, you know whatever he writes about, be it flying or diving in a sub, he has done it.

- What are the machines that are particularly attractive to **Adventurers**?
  _____
  _____

- Are **Adventurers** attracted to military machinery? List some examples.
  _____
  _____

Strategy for Developing/Working with Persons with this Behavior.

If you like machines that produce excitement and are challenging, your best bet is to seek an **Adventurer**. If you loan your car or bike to an **Adventurer**, be sure they are clear about when to return it. **Adventurers** will operate machines better than anyone else.
One way to see if a person is truly an **Adventurer** is to see how he or she handles a machine. Does he or she like to run it and be in control? Is he or she a back seat driver? Is it a temporary activity or a continual style of life?

Do You Have This Behavior? How to Use It to Your Advantage.

If machines are your forte, look for work and occasions where you might use this practical ability. You will receive extra gratification and satisfaction from a slap on the back and appreciation from those concerned. Work within the context of your strengths.

- Ask several **Adventurers** if they like machines? Understand that some **Adventurers** see machines as extensions of themselves. Why would this be?
  _____
  _____

My Career Connection: On the job or in my career I will remember it is the wise **Adventurer** who desires maturity and finally reaches old age who has a plan.

Your Personal Empowerment Statement: Machines are extensions of my hands. I act quickly and precisely in crisis situations.

Color Me Acting Now!

Down with Philosophers

Long philosophical or theoretical arguments bore **Adventurers**. If it works, do it; if it doesn't, move on to something else. **Adventurers** have little interest in what has been or will be. The all-important thing is the eternal now. *Hinc et nunc* (here and now) is the **Adventurers'** motto!

- What is the value of living fully in the present moment rather than waiting for things to get better tomorrow? Why would this approach help you to avoid ulcers?

Strategy for Developing/Working with Persons with this Behavior.

You are doomed to eternal exasperation if you intend to move Adventurers to support any type of cause based on principle rather than action. Wait until you are ready before you call in **Adventurers**.

Do You Have This Behavior? How to Use It to Your Advantage.

Choosing the life style of the soldier of fortune brings certain contempt or sometimes envy from the greater part of society. Be aware of the side effects of your choice.

- Think about the issue of drug involvement. Different personalities are attracted to drugs for different reasons.
- Why would a **Blue** be drawn to drugs?

- Why would a **Red** be drawn to drugs?

- Why would a **Brown** be drawn to drugs?

- Why would a **Green** be drawn to drugs?

If you say **Adventurers** are out for the thrills, **Relaters** want to be with the group, **Builders** love power and **Planners** thrive on inner experiences, you are on the mark. If you were caught by a friend in the act of committing a serious infraction and the friend reported the incident to the authorities, how would you feel about the friend?

My Career Connection: I will seek a job where the action is anchored to today.

Your Personal Empowerment Statement: I always enjoy and relish the present moment.

Call Me Light-Hearted

The More We Get Together, the Happier We'll Be!

Adventurers enjoy others. The togetherness of Adventurers is comradery and not the emotional relating of **Relaters. Adventurers'** reasons for group loyalty are the personal pleasures that it gives. This group loyalty and camaraderie is found in the French Foreign Legion, the military, the fire and police departments and many other fraternal clubs. Such a group lacks the cohesive force of a **Relater** Group. It has been said of old airplanes that they are bunch of nuts and bolts flying in loose formation. The same can be said of **Adventurers** coming together in a group.

- Distinguish between the camaraderie of the **Adventurer** and the emotional attachment of the Relater.

_____
_____
_____

Strategy for Developing/Working with Persons with this Behavior.

The **Adventurers** are excellent people for developing an esprit de corps in any group. They create the fun and excitement that keeps the group vital. If they are suppressed or denied action, they will have a chaotic effect on the group. Be prepared and put on your **Builder** hat.

Do You Have This Behavior? How to Use It to Your Advantage.
Your desire to be the life of the party may be a disaster if it is not party time. Note the difference! Check it out with a **Relater** or **Planner**.

- Identify an **Adventurer** who has been a positive influence in your life. Why?

_____
_____
_____
_____
_____
_____
_____

My Career Connection: I will seek out a job where I can associate with fellow **Adventurers**.

Your Personal Empowerment Statement: When I choose, I easily join in and have a great time with (name or situation).

Call Me Practical.

The Handy-Handyman

Besides their special skills with machines, **Adventurers** usually possess an admirable cool, sobering and practical judgment. Kept on this plane, there is a deliberate, logical follow-through.

Consider the role of paramedics who may go six hours on a shift with no calls, working in a relaxed environment, when suddenly the call comes. The responses must be swift. They don their gear and head to the emergency scene, unaware of what awaits them. Upon their arrival at the scene, they may have to deal with multiple medical emergencies. They must quickly call upon their expertise, equipment and knowledge. Not only does every second count, but so do their actions. They totally accept the challenge of their career as an **Adventurer**.

Ian Fleming created a marvelous **Adventurer** in the form of 007, James Bond. Immediately, we envision lighters that are small bazookas, pens capable of emitting noxious gasses, watches that can do everything from unlocking a cell to blowing away a door. Who else possesses such access to so many incredible vehicles whether they are earth or sky oriented? He is a match for Goldfinger, Mr. Big, and Dr. No!

In Paint Your Wagon, the miners fell upon lean times when the gold ran out. Lee Marvin adapted to the situation. The miners used gold for gambling, liquor, etc., Marvin engineered a network of tunnels under the town's saloons. The idea was to collect all the gold dust that had fallen through the floor boards. "Whatever will be, will be!" This practical acceptance of reality was further illustrated when Lee Marvin showed complete indifference to the destruction of the town when the earth started caving in under the buildings. One of Hollywood's best special effects sequences followed: all the buildings of the entire gold-boom town started crashing to the ground. Marvin walked on, unconcerned and expressionless, through the town as a chain reaction of crashing and undermined buildings fell on every side of him.

A wild, escaped bull decides that Marvin would be an excellent object to gore. The sequences of crashing buildings, caving in tunnels and a bull chasing Marvin are hilarious, but it should be noted that only when the action began with the bull chasing Marvin, did he really move. Some might call this reckless behavior. It is a tendency **Adventurers** need to be aware of within themselves. Consider the career of Kelly Flynn, the first female Air Force officer to pilot the B-52. Her expertise put her in the cockpit. Her recklessness in her personal life cost her a career.

- Why is the practical judgment of an **Adventurer** an asset in fields such as paramedics, the military, law enforcement and fire control?

_____
_____
_____

Strategy for Developing/Working with Persons with this Behavior.

If you are to be successful in any action crisis or need a practical sober judgment, get the **Adventurers** involved. You will be forced to throw out all the theory and get down to what actually works in the real world.

- Have you ever experienced a situation where an **Adventurer** saved the day? Explain.

_____
_____

Do You Have This Behavior? How to Use It to Your Advantage.

If you like to have people appreciate your ability in practical matters and your know-how in times of crisis, take advantage of this gift. Make sure that you do not throw the baby out with the bath water, as winging it all the time may lead to disaster. Have a **Planner** handy at least to test your intentions. You may build a house on the side of a mountain, and the rains will wash everything down to the canyon in a few hours. A prime example of this is the building of mountain-clinging homes by adventurous entrepreneurs in Southern California.

- Check out your action plans with a **Builder** if you wish to build an empire, with a **Planner** if you wish to avoid mistakes and with a **Relater** if you wish people to like and appreciate you.

My Career Connection: I will seek a career where calculated risk-taking is an option.

Your Personal Empowerment Statement: I take pride in my practical judgment of (situation) which is right on target.

*Excellence is to do a common thing
in an uncommon way*
                -Booker T. Washington

The Adult Adventurer in Summary

When you were born you came with a skateboard attached and a glove on your hand. You would have preferred a trapeze hanging over your bassinet instead of a mobile. It took you no time at all to figure out how to escape from your crib. Floor vents were for storage. Toys were created to be disassembled so you could examine what made them work. If a toy made no noise, you became a sound specialist. Toilets were test sites. How many different objects could be flushed? Carl the Rottweiler created by Alexandra Day was your hero. His entire life was an adventure.

Monkey bars served as frameworks for constructing clubhouses. If height was involved like Edmond Hillary on Mt. Everest, you climbed it because it was there. Barn rooftops were for jumping off. Your parents called it not using your head. You called it flying. The doctor called it a split lip, bitten tongue and lucky. Probably by the age of seven your parents had condemned your room as a war zone. Middle school was a wake up call. Maybe the opposite sex had some interesting attributes. Doing projects or assignments ahead of schedule didn't make a lot of sense to you when they could be done the night before they were due.

Your locker in high school, in all likelihood, became an archeological site filled with old lunch sacks, overdue library books, athletic equipment the coach was still looking for from two seasons ago, half of your clothes, multiple textbooks you had garnered along the way, and unfinished projects. You learned the hard way that subtlety over bluntness worked better in relationships. While you liked to do things on the spur of the moment you learned that the spontaneous approach was not the motivation of **Builders**, **Planners** and **Relater**s. Regarding a career choice, you were sure that you didn't want it to be boring.

The **ADVENTURER** in you has always been action focused. Action is your passion. You do not enjoy sitting on the bench unless it is a necessity. Consider fire fighting or being a SWAT team member. Professional athletics, testing sports equipment or coaching are great outlets. The greater the odds against reaching your goal, the better your response. It's most exciting when John Elway is down six points with 18 seconds left to win the game.

You would rather be racing downhill against the clock than designing the skis you are wearing. The floor of the New York Stock Exchange is just another sports arena. Exporting and importing will have appeal if they involve travel. A ramp leads to a 360 in the air on a skateboard. A stage isn't for viewing, but for acting, choreography, or creating the barricade from *Les Miserables*.

You are tactile. For you, touch is sensuous whether it is the feel of a niche in a wall of rock you are scaling, a piece of wood you are carving, a musical drum stick, a throttle beneath your foot, a power level in your hand or clay on a wheel. You have always known that learning while sitting in rows is on a par with sitting in a vat of wet concrete. Your brain literally closes down. Think back on classes where learning came easily for you. Did they involve participation, hands on projects, exhibitions? If your answer is yes, be sure to take your style into account as you go about the process of selecting or changing careers. Louis Nizer said, "A man who works with his hands is a laborer; a man who works with his hands and his brain is a craftsman; but a man who works with his hands and his brain and his heart is an artist." He could have been describing you sculpting, carding and weaving wool, tearing down an engine and rebuilding it, playing a guitar or being a chef.

Being a disk jockey, a radio talk host, an on site radio or television reporter, a 911 dispatcher or telemarketer comes easily to you. While the above careers may require strange working hours this will not be a challenge to you. Kemmons Wilson, CEO for Holiday Inns, sums up the internal clock of an **Adventurer**: "I like to work half a day. I don't care if it's the first twelve hours or the second twelve hours. I just put in my half every day. It keeps me out of trouble."

Spontaneity is natural to you. You think on your feet. This strength can get you in trouble with **Builder** and **Planner** rules if you do not remember to accommodate when necessary. As an **Adventurer**, you will create the fun in an otherwise boring process. It is a quality that will be a godsend on any job. You make a great comedian. Study Robin Williams, Elaine Boosler, Jerry Seinfeld, Joan Rivers, Bill Cosby, Will Rogers, Ellen DeGeneres, Bob Hope, Jack Benny, Roseanne Barr, Billy Crystal, Phyllis Diller, Jay Leno, Gilda Radner, Bill Murray, Phil Hartman, Jane Curtin, Paula Poundstone, Dana Carvey, Steve Martin, Lily Tomlin, Rosie O'Donnell, John Candy and Joy Behr. You have probably been performing for years helping us to find the humor in a day. The **Adventurer** is often undervalued by the other personalities as being frivolous and not very serious. Remember, we frequently live vicariously through your actions and gift for laughter.

"Carpe Diem" --- Seize the Day is your motto. You live in the present. Yesterday is gone and you will deal with tomorrow when it comes. Today is what counts. Relish it. Use it as you will. Either go all out 100% or just sit back and watch the sun set. To paraphrase Diane Ackerman, "(You) don't want to get to the end of (your) life and find that (you) just lived the length of it. (You) want to have lived the width of it as well." Your ability to sit back and let the world revolve on its axis makes you not only unique, but an enigma to the other colors. The **Planner** will perceive your actions as rebellious. The **Builder** will conclude that you are just being irresponsible and lazy. The **Relater** will be concerned by what appears to be your withdrawal from the interaction of daily life. You are neither rebellious, irresponsible nor withdrawn. You are simply taking a break and not only reducing your stress level but enjoying the beauty of a sunset. It is this attitude that keeps you from becoming a candidate for stress related diseases. As an **Adventurer**, there are times when you do not comprehend the motivation of **Builders** or **Planners**, believing both are too serious and intense. To you the **Relater** is too focused on people and lacks excitement. Be patient. Teach them to incorporate "red" into their daily lives. Remember, however, the **Adventurer** can and will make a plan for tomorrow if the payoff is **Adventure** tomorrow. You just won't make a plan for the sake of a plan.

Float in a canoe
  Let evening enfold, drift
    Through hot night diamonds
            ---Shay

Excitement is your lifeblood. The Adventurer and a lack of confidence are mutually exclusive. When written in Chinese, the word "crisis" is composed of two characters. One represents danger, and the other represents opportunity. An E.R. physician or nurse, a paramedic, the secret service, border patrol, security or a NASA payload specialist are careers where you will excel. Your spontaneity is an asset in these career areas. The Adventurer in you thrives on challenge. You don't like failure but you do not fear it. You are pragmatic. You recognize that the risk of failure comes with the territory when you take on a challenge. Failure for a **Builder** is connected to ego while it is personal loss to the **Planner**. For you it doesn't have the same destructive effect. You will not seek it out, but if it does occur, you won't agonize over it. Instead you will either move on or retrench. Blaming others is not your style. Louis Nizer was speaking for you when he said, " When a man points a finger at someone else, he should remember that four of his fingers are pointing at himself."

Boundaries and walls are confining unless you are crossing them, scaling them or erecting them. The standard office in most cases will have a smothering effect on you. You need the opportunity to work in changing environments or the out-of-doors. Investigate ecology, wildlife preservation, agriculture and photography. You would rather be photographing the migration of polar bears than just reading about it. Consider the professions of construction and contracting, forestry, oceanography, marine biology, geology, topology and surveying call out to your **Adventurer** spirit. Read up on the backgrounds of Clive Cussler or Tom Clancy and learn how a person can combine a love of adventure with writing. Subscribe to National Geographic. If unlocking keys to the past appeals to you then consider anthropology and archeology. You find repetitive structure and routine boring. Consequently, you more easily accommodate to an irregular workday than the **Builder, Planner** and **Relater**.

<u>Some measure of risk is most often a requirement</u>. Red Adair found the burning oil fields of Kuwait an acceptable level of risk. He knew what he was doing. The flight deck of an aircraft carrier for the men and women of the Navy is an acceptable risk. If they do their jobs right, no one will get hurt. Some of you will find appeal in deep sea diving, underwater salvage, off-shore drilling and platform construction. Add to that list cave spelunking, vulcanology, high wire rigging, racing cars, hydroplanes or horse racing and your motivation is up and running. Icarus with his wings of feathers and wax and Orville and Wilbur Wright understood. Today you are every bush pilot, crop duster, med-air-vac pilot, military and commercial aviator and test pilot. As John Glenn on February 20, 1962, you left the earth in Friendship 7, orbited the earth three times and launched the U.S. space program. On July 20, 1969, Neil Armstrong made his first steps on the moon surface and summed up the experience when he said, "That's one small step for a man, one giant leap for mankind."

As an **Adventurer** the following two responses to such a momentous event will make sense to you.

> "Treading the soil of the moon, palpating its pebbles, tasting the panic and splendor of the event, feeling in the pit of one's stomach the separation from terra . . . these form the most romantic sensation an explorer has ever known . . .this is the only thing I can say about the matter. The utilitarian results do not interest me."
>
> ---Arthur Koestler (1905-83)
> Hungarian-born British author

> "So there he is at last. Man on the moon. The poor magnificent bungler! He can't even get to the office without undergoing the agonies of the damned, but give him a little metal, a few chemicals, some wire and twenty or thirty billion dollars and, vroom! There he is, up on a rock a quarter of a million miles up in the sky."
>
> ---Russell Baker (1925-)
> U.S. journalist

Astronauts represent an outstanding example of balancing the **Adventurer** motivation with the vision of the **Planner** and the drive of the **Builder**. With the selection of the first astronauts, the public embraced them and in that embracing placed them in the spotlight. Their personal lives became the focus of our attention. Recognizing they were the ambassadors of NASA, they had to draw upon their **Relater** skills. Visit any astronaut web site today and you will find them demonstrating all four strengths. Remember, the **Adventurer** is not without a plan. If the motivation is to become an astronaut or a scientist then the rigors of earning a Ph.D. will be met.

One of your authors followed the space program from its inception with the Mercury project. Such names as Shepard, Grissom, Glenn, Carpenter, Schirra and Cooper, part of the Mercury project, are ingrained in her memory. After Mercury came Gemini and Apollo. The loss of Grissom, White and Chaffee who died in a fire on the Apollo launch pad served to remind all of us that danger and risk were inherent in such a young program. As James Lovell and his crew battled to find their way back home from 200,000 miles in space, time crawled. When Apollo 13 splashed down the entire world cheered. We were back on track. Our **Adventurers** had returned unscathed. Watching space shuttle *Columbia* launch and successfully land, piloted by Young and Crippen at Edwards Air Force base was incredible. Launch followed launch and we grew complacent about the space program. And then in 1983, with classrooms across the nation watching, waiting to see the first teacher, Christa McAuliffe, enter space, the risk factor was devastatingly driven home. We watched in disbelief as *Challenger*, 73 seconds into launch, exploded, taking the lives of Scobee, Smith, Resnik, Onizuka, McNair, Jarvis and McAuliffe. Never again, we vowed, would we take a shuttle launch as a given. But time is a strange healer. For almost three years we waited and then on September 29, 1988, the 26th mission of the space shuttle roared successfully into space. The spirit of the **Adventurer** had been returned to us as a nation.

When this co-author began her research for this section she could remember the 7th mission when Sally Ride was a part of the crew. She had a general recall of regular announcements of shuttle launches taking communication satellites into space, low keyed defense missions, the Hubble Telescope, scientific projects and the link-ups with a troubled MIR. So how many missions had there been to date? How many astronauts had traveled to that point in orbit where "We" became small, blue and beautiful and floating in space? What would you guess?

Through July 2001 there have been 104 space shuttle missions. Ten more missions have been planned to date. This author was almost staggered by how many launches she had missed. She could have spent several days at the NASA website. Including Mercury, Gemini and Apollo, 631 men and 78 women of NASA have entered space. What is even more amazing is how many of those astronauts have returned not just once, twice, three times, but four times, five times (Lucid, Gibson & Blaha) and the indomitable Story Musgrave who flew his 6th and last mission (November 19 – December 7, 1996) retiring in 1997 at the age of 62.

Take a few minutes and read the following biographical information on Story Musgrave and experience an astronaut who balanced his **Adventurer** motivation with the motivations of the **Builder, Planner** and **Relater**.

NASA Astronaut Story Musgrave

PERSONAL DATA:

Born August 19, 1935, in Boston, Massachusetts, but considers Lexington, Kentucky, to be his hometown. Single. Six children (one deceased). His hobbies are chess, flying, gardening, literary criticism, microcomputers, parachuting, photography, reading, running, scuba diving, and soaring.

EDUCATION:

Graduated from St. Mark's School, Southborough, Massachusetts, in 1953; received a bachelor of science degree in mathematics and statistics from Syracuse University in 1958, a master of business administration degree in operations analysis and computer programming from the University of California at Los Angeles in 1959, a bachelor of arts degree in chemistry from Marietta College in 1960, a doctorate in medicine from Columbia University in 1964, a master of science in physiology and biophysics from the University of Kentucky in 1966, and a master of arts in literature from the University of Houston in 1987.

ORGANIZATIONS:

Member of Alpha Kappa Psi, the American Association for the Advancement of Science, Beta Gamma Sigma, the Civil Aviation Medical Association, the Flying Physicians Association, the International Academy of Astronautics, the Marine Corps Aviation Association, the National Aeronautic Association, the National Aerospace Education Council, the National Geographic Society, the Navy League, the New York Academy of Sciences, Omicron Delta Kappa, Phi Delta Theta, the Soaring Club of Houston, the Soaring Society of America, and the United States Parachute Association.

SPECIAL HONORS:

National Defense Service Medal and an Outstanding Unit Citation as a member of the United States Marine Corps Squadron VMA-212 (1954); United States Air Force Post-doctoral Fellowship (1965-1966); National Heart Institute Post-doctoral Fellowship (1966-1967); Reese Air Force Base Commander's Trophy (1969); American College of Surgeons I.S. Ravdin Lecture (1973); NASA Exceptional Service Medals (1974 & 1986); Flying Physicians Association Airman of the Year

Award (1974 & 1983); NASA Space Flight Medals (1983, 1985, 1989, 1991, 1993, 1996); NASA Distinguished Service Medal (1992).

EXPERIENCE:

Musgrave entered the United States Marine Corps in 1953, served as an aviation electrician and instrument technician, and as an aircraft crew chief while completing duty assignments in Korea, Japan, Hawaii, and aboard the carrier USS Wasp in the Far East.

He has flown 17,700 hours in 160 different types of civilian and military aircraft, including 7,500 hours in jet aircraft. He has earned FAA ratings for instructor, instrument instructor, glider instructor, and airline transport pilot, and U.S. Air Force Wings. An accomplished parachutist, he has made more than 500 free falls -- including over 100 experimental free-fall descents involved with the study of human aerodynamics.

Dr. Musgrave was employed as a mathematician and operations analyst by the Eastman Kodak Company, Rochester, New York, during 1958.

He served a surgical internship at the University of Kentucky Medical Center in Lexington from 1964 to 1965, and continued there as a U. S. Air Force post-doctoral fellow (1965-1966), working in aerospace medicine and physiology, and as a National Heart Institute post-doctoral fellow (1966-1967), teaching and doing research in cardiovascular and exercise physiology. From 1967 to 1989, he continued clinical and scientific training as a part-time surgeon at the Denver General Hospital and as a part-time professor of physiology and biophysics at the University of Kentucky Medical Center.

He has written 25 scientific papers in the areas of aerospace medicine and physiology, temperature regulation, exercise physiology, and clinical surgery.

NASA EXPERIENCE:

Dr. Musgrave was selected as a scientist-astronaut by NASA in August 1967. He completed astronaut academic training and then worked on the design and development of the *Skylab* Program. He was the backup science-pilot for the first Skylab mission, and was a CAPCOM for the second and third *Skylab* missions. Dr. Musgrave participated in the design and development of all Space Shuttle extravehicular activity equipment including spacesuits, life support systems, airlocks, and manned maneuvering units. From 1979 to 1982, and 1983 to 1984, he was assigned as a test and verification pilot in the Shuttle Avionics Integration Laboratory at JSC. He served as a spacecraft communicator (CAPCOM) for STS-31, STS-35, STS-36, STS-38 and STS-41, and lead CAPCOM for a number of subsequent flights. He was a mission specialist on STS-6 in 1983, STS-51F/Spacelab-2 in 1985, STS-33 in 1989 and STS-44 in 1991, was the payload commander on STS-61 in 1993, and a mission specialist on STS-80 in 1996. A veteran of six space flights, Dr. Musgrave has spent a total of 1,281 hours 59 minutes, 22 seconds in space. Dr. Musgrave left NASA in August 1997 to pursue private interests.

SPACE FLIGHT EXPERIENCE:

Dr. Musgrave first flew on STS-6, which launched from the Kennedy Space Center, Florida, on April 4, 1983, and landed at Edwards Air Force Base, California, on April 9, 1983. During this maiden voyage of Space Shuttle *Challenger*, the crew performed the first Shuttle deployment of an IUS/TDRS satellite, and Musgrave and Don Peterson conducted the first Space Shuttle extravehicular activity (EVA) to test the new space suits and construction and repair devices and procedures. Mission duration was 5 days, 23 minutes, 42 seconds.

On STS-51F/Spacelab-2, the crew aboard *Challenger* launched from the Kennedy Space Center, Florida, on July 29, 1985, and landed at Edwards Air Force Base, California, on August 6, 1985. This flight was the first pallet-only Spacelab mission, and the first mission to operate the Spacelab Instrument Pointing System (IPS). It carried 13 major experiments in astronomy, astrophysics, and life sciences. During this mission, Dr. Musgrave served as the systems engineer during launch and entry, and as a pilot during the orbital operations. Mission duration was 7 days, 22 hours, 45 minutes, 26 seconds.

On STS-33, he served aboard the Space Shuttle *Discovery*, which launched at night from the Kennedy Space Center, Florida, on November 22, 1989. This classified mission operated payloads for the Department of Defense. Following 79 orbits, the mission concluded on November 27, 1989, with a landing at sunset on Runway 04 at Edwards Air Force Base, California. Mission duration was 5 days, 7 minutes, 32 seconds.

STS-44 also launched at night on November 24, 1991. The primary mission objective was accomplished with the successful deployment of a Defense Support Program (DSP) satellite with an Inertial Upper Stage (IUS) rocket booster. In addition the crew also conducted two Military Man in Space Experiments, three radiation monitoring experiments, and numerous medical tests to support longer duration Shuttle flights. The mission was concluded in 110 orbits of the Earth with *Atlantis* returning to a landing on the lakebed at Edwards Air Force Base, California, on December 1, 1991. Mission duration was 6 days, 22 hours, 50 minutes, 42 seconds.

STS-61 was the first Hubble Space Telescope (HST) servicing and repair mission. Following a night launch from Kennedy Space Center on December 2, 1993, the Endeavour rendezvoused with and captured the HST. During this 11-day flight, the HST was restored to its full capabilities through the work of two pairs of astronauts during a record 5 spacewalks. Dr. Musgrave performed 3 of these spacewalks. After having traveled 4,433,772 miles in 163 orbits of the Earth, *Endeavour* returned to a night landing in Florida on December 13, 1993. Mission duration was 10 days, 19 hours, 59 minutes.

On STS-80 (November 19 to December 7, 1996), the crew aboard Space Shuttle *Columbia* deployed and retrieved the Wake Shield Facility (WSF) and the Orbiting Retrievable Far and Extreme Ultraviolet Spectrometer (ORFEUS) satellites. The free-flying WSF created a super vacuum in its wake in which to grow thin film wafers for use in semiconductors and the electronics industry. The ORFEUS instruments, mounted on the reusable Shuttle Pallet Satellite, studied the origin and makeup of stars. In completing this mission he logged a record 278 earth orbits, traveled over 7 million miles in 17 days, 15 hours, 53 minutes.

You have just met a legend from the 20th century!

Women have flown on board the shuttle 74 times as of July 2001. Women like Dr. Sally Ride (first American woman in space), Eileen Collins (1st pilot and 1st shuttle commander), Bonnie Dunbar (16.8 million miles in space over the course of 4 missions), Shannon Lucid (5 months aboard MIR and the only woman to ever receive the Congressional Space Medal of Honor) have opened the door for their fellow female astronauts.

In October of 1998, Senator John Glenn at the age of 76, became the oldest person to travel in space aboard the Space Shuttle *Discovery* on a ten-day mission. What sets you apart as an **Adventurer** is how you define "risk." A.J. Foyt stated he felt safer on a race track than on the Houston freeway. For the astronauts of NASA their track just happens to be the universe.

You will get things done with little waste of time. Committee decisions are not for you if they involve either the **Planner** or the **Relater**. Remember, there will be times when you need to accommodate the motivations of the other colors if you want to achieve your goals. The Nike campaign "Just Do it!" could have been written by you. When something goes off line, gets screwed up, instead of first looking for the fault you will seek to expedite its correction. Afterwards you can enjoy the challenge of seeking out the cause. It is this quality that makes you a great troubleshooter in computer technology. You are a visionary in your ability to see alternative approaches. This talent will be an asset if you opt for architecture, arbitration or labor management.

You are a natural entrepreneur. You will follow the star you create. Steven Spielberg is a wonderful example of a **Planner** with an **Adventurer** back-up. Prolific creativity and risk-taking perhaps best describe him. Take a moment and review his list of films. It is like reading a chapter in American history.

1941, Jaws, Close Encounters of the Third Kind, Blues Brothers, E.T. The Extra-Terrestrial, Poltergeist, Raiders of the Lost Ark, Indiana Jones and the Temple of Doom, Back to the Future, Young Sherlock Holmes, The Goonies, The Color Purple, An American Tail, Empire of the Sun, Batteries Not Included, Who Framed Roger Rabbit, The Land Before Time, Always, Indiana Jones and the Last Crusade, Back to the Future II, Rollercoaster Rabbit, Back to the Future III, Tiny Toon Adventures, Joe Versus the Volcano, Gremlins II:The New Batch, Hook, An American Tail: Fievel Goes West, The Magical World of Chuck Jones, TinyToon Adventures: How I Spent My Vacation, Jurassic Park, Schindler's List, We're Back: A Dinosaur's Tale, Animaniacs, The Family Dog, The Flintstones, Casper, Balto, Pinky and the Brain, Freakazoid, Twister, The Lost World, Men in Black, Amistad, Deep Impact, The Mask of Zorro, Saving Private Ryan, Memoirs of a Geisha, Jurassic Park 3, Indiana Jones, Other Films.

By 1997, Spielberg's annual income reached $283 million, making him the highest paid entertainment figure of that year. How was he able to achieve such a mark? His skills as an entrepreneur combined with his inventiveness and artistry were a driving force.
- In 1982 he founded *Amblin*, a production studio, with a current $400 million value (100% ownership).
- In 1994 in partnership with Katzenberg and Geffen, he helped found *Dreamworks* SKG, the first new movie studio in Hollywood in over 75 years. $550 Million value (22% ownership).

- *Dive*! A restaurant chain. $6 million value. (50% ownership).
- *Idealab*! Internet content. $7.5 million value. (15% ownership).

The source of the following quote is unknown but it epitomizes the entrepreneur **Adventurer**:

"The people who get on in this world are the people who get up and look for the circumstances they want, and, if they can't find them, make them."

Celebrate your sense of **Adventure**. Without it and without you, this would be a boring world.

Your Communication Key (action):

Build an atmosphere of freedom of action, excitement and fun

Your secret vocabulary for

- developing **Adventurer** behaviors

- getting along with persons with strong **ADVENTURER** behaviors:

  * fun * excitement * spend * adventure * spontaneous *

  * action * machines * gamble * fun * chance * games *

  * quick * fast * change * act out * joke * entrepreneur *

ADVENTURER - RED

Build an atmosphere of freedom of action.

Comfort zone: Action, unstructured work situations; movers; prefers procedures that are useful, dynamic, practical and hands-on; importance of spontaneity; here and now are important; be on stage; touch

Demands on others: Action oriented - spontaneous responses - respond quickly to curves - be competitive - be on stage at a moment's notice - pick up the pieces - fun and light-hearted attitude, take a joke

How to build powerful teams, self-esteem, success,
maximum productivity in others and reinforce leadership.

* HOT BUTTONS *

When the **Adventurer (red) part of self** in a person is very strong,
consider what motivates that person and apply it.

- Take a light-hearted, fun or action approach to **Adventurers'** communications.
- Speak to the here and now.
- Be as flexible as they are to changing action, be careful of the action's direction.
- Direct spontaneous action towards positive goals or you will be one of the major sources for encouraging turnover, delinquency or criminal actions.
- Involve them in any positive action situation. Be careful not to get caught in the thrill.
- Create result-oriented action situations according to the family's, club's, company's or organization's goals.
- Allow them to play a "starring" role on any occasion possible.
- Check and make sure they are in positive action situations, provide exercise areas and home, work, recreational or social occasions to let off steam.

Hot Button Value

Why give our attention to the Secret Vocabulary or to the Hot Buttons covered for the Planner on page 70, for the Builder on page 107, for the Relater on page 147 and the Adventurer on page 188? You have identified your own strengths but others do not recognize your strengths because they have not been exposed to this process. So they are not going to adjust to your values in communication. Theoretically, one out of four people will have the same strength as you – and you will find it easy to communicate with them.

The only option is for you to adjust to the strengths of others. How do you identify their strengths?

Demeanour is defined as outward behavior, conduct, manner, deportment, air, bearing. We can just call them clues. In addition to these, what words are used?

It would be convenient if others used the words on these lists promptly to provide clues for us. They do not always help us by doing this. They will, however, provide instant clues in their desk organization, office surroundings, or in their attention to dress. Their mannerisms may also provide clues. The key is we need to not only listen but to also be observant.

Our life experiences in relating with others give us an automatic use of our language in a give and take, answer and reply, or corresponding and responding. The use of the **Winning Colors®** process, however, provides an easy understanding handle and a pre-planned idea of the change necessary to quickly and purposefully adjust to the strength of the person with whom we are communicating.

As a **BROWN BUILDER**, I may try to push the exchange along to a more brief, concise, bottom line conclusion. Another **BROWN BUILDER** will go along with my direction in the communication. A **GREEN PLANNER** will most certainly hold back from my communication intent, and by implication will keep the exchange going for more examination of details and process in exploring the idea. The **BROWN BUILDER** can overpower and drive on to the concise conclusion and end the exchange. How will that leave the **GREEN PLANNER**?

The **RED ADVENTURER** will display physical clues. The exchange will be quicker, perhaps implying less thoughtful communication. There will be more physical movement, and more interjection of fun into the comments. The **BLUE RELATER** will bring personal interest into the exchange. Whatever the exchange, the value of the ideas will be connected to people, or groups, or the social nature in a harmonious manner.

In identifying the strengths of others, I can easily check my instant opinion by framing my communication around the words on these lists. The response of the others will show you whether your early identification was correct. If not, simply adjust accordingly.

Adjusting to the strengths of others will provide you with a communication foundation based on like communication values.

BOW! WOW!

When one is dealing with different behavioral strengths, it becomes necessary to speak that person's language if communication is to take place. Consider the story of the mother mouse and her young who came upon a cat. The cat's response was to immediately assume the crouch position ready to spring, his tongue quickly flicking back and forth anticipating hors oeuvres to the main course. The mother mouse stepped forth, drew herself up and let fly a marvelous roaring BOW! WOW! The cat executed an immediate 180 degree turn and took off at a dead run. The mother mouse turned to her young and, smiling gently, said, "It is good to know another's language!"

In our opinion, one should consider this mother mouse for the diplomatic corps. She understood that while in Spain, one speaks Spanish; while in France, one speaks French; and when dealing with different behavioral styles of the **Adventurer, Relater, Builder** and **Planner** speak the languages of **Red, Blue, Brown** and **Green**.

A Bad Dream or a Nightmare?

Mirror on the wall who is the worst leader of all? As you read through the following list, think back on the number of leadership types you have experienced during your life's journey. Check any you recognize. Feel free to add your own examples.

- ❏ **The Usurper.** This type of leader takes credit for all contributions. If a paper is to be presented or submitted to a journal the Usurpers name will be at the top of the list whether or not he possesses knowledge of the subject matter.

- ❏ **Poison Pen.** Present a file for review to Mr.Hyde and Dr. Jeykle picks up the pen. Positive comments are a waste of time.

- ❏ **Emotionally Attached.** Had one good idea 20 years ago. All other new ideas or creations must take their place in line.

- ❏ **A Little Knowledge is a Dangerous Thing.** Try to introduce a new idea and you will be confronted with the standard phrase of "Research says . . . ." It doesn't matter whether the research is obscure, out of date or not applicable.

- ❏ **Throw It Against the Wall.** Quantity not quality is the driving force. Just get the finished product out into the market place.

- ❏ **The Nitpicker.** The U.S. Constitution . . ."too many loop holes." The Taj Mahal . . . "overdone." St. Basils . . . " too much woodworking." Two page report . . . "too long."

- ❏ **We and They.** If you agree with me, you are on the "we" team.

- ❏ **A Boiling Caldron.** Lets you know through body language and tone of voice that you are in the presence of an impending uncontrollable explosion. If you just go along, the volcano will continue to rest quietly just beneath the surface.

- ❏ **Challenge My Ideas, You Challenge Me.**

- ❏ **Memo Master #1.** Issues 4-page single spaced memos to be read prior to meetings. Considers them decrees not open to discussion.

- ❏ **Memo Master #2.** Issues 4-page single spaced memos to be read prior to meetings. Reads them aloud at meetings.

- ❏ **The Meeting Addict.** Holds daily or weekly meetings whether they are necessary or not.Be assured the idea of a 10-20 minute meeting does not exist in his/her repertoire.

- ❏ **If You Can't Be Seen, You Must Not Be Working.** Sometimes desk placement is on a par with a prison guard watchtower. The idea of some staff working at home or being independents in the field drives this leader almost to distraction.

- **Public Relations.** Total focus is image. The hull of the ship may be rotting beneath the waterline, but if what is visible looks good, then everything is fine.

- **Defers all Decisions.** Wants a clean slate in the managerial climb. Never puts his or her signature on anything open to question. Motto is "Let Mikey eat it." If Mickey is successful then will claim credit.

- **Won't Risk.** All responses begin with "But, what if . . ."

- **Just One Big Family.** And family works as many hours as are needed, including weekends. Results are what counts. Salaries are secondary. Strangely, no one is standing in line to be formally adopted.

- **I Am the Leader and Never Forget It!** As if you could.

- **The Story Teller.** Lives in the past. Believes the "kids" of today lack the work ethic.

- **King or Queen of the Buzz Words.** New buzzwords or phrases will be used like a buzz saw. (acronyms)

- **One Up-man-ship.** Any ideas new ideas or innovations are greeted with, "Been there, done that and better."

- **Made It to the Top and Forgot Everything Along the Way.** Talks the talk of having risen out of the trenches, but has no recall or empathy for those still working at lower levels.

- **Acquired a University Degree and Stopped Learning.** Hasn't read a professional journal or current text in the last 10-15 years. When challenged, always cites out of date experts.

- **The Socializer.** Believes everyone should not only work together, but also socialize together. Doesn't understand why the sign-ups for company picnics and potluck dinners aren't 100%.

- **Keep Them Down on the Farm.** Coffee breaks are 15-minute meetings. Lunch is delivered to individual desks. Short of Medic One, no one leaves the premises during working hours.

- **The Prince or Princess of Platitudes.** "You don't have to work longer hours, just work smarter." "Do more with less." "No pain, no gain." Perhaps the employee gain is based on the pain of listening to such platitudes

- **In Charge of Hindsight.** Imposes the template of hindsight on any decision that does not pan out 100%.

- **Master or Mistress of Gotcha.** Comes into work early or stays late focusing on quality control. You arrive in the morning and before you have even taken off your coat you find yourself answering a list of questions. This person either does not comprehend the need for transition time or chooses to disregard it completely. Even Mr. Rogers is allowed time to take off his jacket, put on his sweater and change his shoes before he begins his show.

- **The Attacker.** Considers his or her contributions or ideas are inviolate. You suggest the need for reconsideration. You find yourself the target of personal attack.

- **Goodnik.** Defers all confrontations or correctives to second in command or support staff. No trace of fingerprints will be found at the scene, but all know whom the gloves fit.

Can you think of any other styles?

- _____
_____

_____
_____

_____
_____

So How Do You Deal With a Bad Dream or Nightmare in the Form of a Leader?

It has been said, an ounce of prevention is worth a pound of cure. Speaking the language of such leaders, understanding their motivation and being prepared are key factors.

The Usuper. Document your contributions. Keep a file. Know there will come a time when the **Usuper** will be questioned regarding the content of the paper, either in written form or at a conference. If you are lucky, you may be present. Don't rush to the rescue. Bide your time. You will know when to make your Builder/Planner entrance.

Poison Pen. Once again, put your response in writing. Add your response to the file. If this is not possible, keep your own file for review time. Too many of us, write this person off and fail to respond. Such actions are on a par with digging one's own grave. Know the business graveyard is filled with Relaters and Planners who elected to avoid a confrontation.

Emotionally Attached. You can choose to either work around this person or you can openly ask, "Are you emotionally attached to this idea or project?" Listen carefully by bringing up your Blue for exterior detail and your Green for interior detail. The attachment may be to only one point or a minor detail. Once you understand the attachment you can skillfully and diplomatically incorporate it. If it is the entire project, you will probably find yourself sitting on a log jam where the concept of team does not exist. At this point check out your own emotional attachments as well as other team members. One Middle East crisis is enough.

A Little Knowledge is a Dangerous Thing. Be prepared. Move into the Planner mode. Support your new idea with current research and documentation. Make copies of your resources or have them with you.

Throw It Against the Wall. Bring up your Brown and Green. Hold firm to your position. Remember your name will be at the top of the list if failure should occur.

The Nitpicker. It is time for a multiple approach. Present your idea in Builder/Adventurer form and Planner form. Staple the Builder/Adventurer approach on top and the Planner addendum underneath.

We and They. Every team needs rules. All must agree to the concept there is no "We and They." The use of the term "They" diminishes. When the term is used, confront it immediately. More than one war has been lost because the term "They" was used. When no face is attached, there is the tendency to underestimate.

A Boiling Caldron. Put on your emotional flak jacket. If necessary, allow the volcano to spew. When the spewing is done, restate your position calmly and quietly. If the volcano isn't done, step back and let the lava flow. After that with firm authority address the issue. Remember, even volcanoes have to take a break now and then to gather up energy. Obviously, if the situation is physically threatening--- Leave!

Challenge My Ideas, You Challenge Me. This may be a matter of super ego or major out of sight insecurities. Put your Blues and Greens together and see if they can determine the source. If you challenge this leader's authority, be sure to send in the Builders and Adventurers. Include a Relater for the sake of seeking harmony.

Memo Master #1. Entitlement is the issue in this situation. Bring up your Red or Green. Ask, "Why?" This type of leader may respond with "There is no need for discussion" or "This is not the time." Keep asking "Why?" Know that along the way, others will be empowered by your actions to join you. When more than one "Why'" enters the fray, you have reached team discussion.

Memo Master #2. Approach this problem with your Relater skills. Offer to divide the memo up. Have each color summarize and present a section. Explain you want to share the load. If agreement is reached, be sure each presenter gives credit to the originator of the memo. No matter what color we are, we all want recognition.

The Meeting Addict. How many of us have lost an entire morning or afternoon in a meeting that could have been summed up in 10-20 minutes. We walk back to our desks, grumbling, "Could have done that in half the time or in a memo." Listen closely and identify those grumblers who are Brown or Red. Make it a challenge. Ask if any of them would be willing to lead the next meeting. If leadership is not shared, you will have to negotiate. Send a Brown and a Red to negotiate. Once your team has experienced an efficient 10-20 minute meeting they will be converted. Set a time limit.

If You Can't Be Seen, You Must Not Be Working. This is a tough one. Some leaders just have to be in the watchtower. More and more computers are making in the field work or at home a reality. Bring up you Green and document everything you do. If you are confronted, you will have the records. Remember the finished product will not contain a record of the time you invested.

Public Relations. If your leader is an over the edge Blue whose strength lies in public relations and nothing else, build a strong balanced support team. The team members will have to put on their scuba suits and focus on repairing and shoring up the hull of the ship. Know this type of leader will be glad to avoid such details. Be sure to have your Blues monitoring the public image as you effect change.

Defers All Decisions. There are those in mid-management who just will not put their names on anything that might be open to question. They agonize when confronted. Send the Planners in first to test the waters. Is it detail that is needed? If this is the situation, the Planners will prevail with their patience. If they fail, change tactics.

With this type of leader, pick your wars. Be the first to put your position in writing. Remember it takes energy to tell you why you are wrong. Move through the hierarchy carefully. If the situation is vital take a Builder stand. Make copies of your proposal. When the time comes and you are confronted by upper management, you will be ready. It won't be pleasant in all likelihood, but remember the line, "Place the blame, Mame."

Won't Risk. When dealing with The "But, what if . . . ?" leader, call on your Planners. They will have the tenacity and understanding. Planners can empathize with such a position. Just remember to set a deadline.

Just One Big Family. It has been said, "We can't choose our family, but thank God, we can choose our friends." The same is true of employment. There are many successful family ventures that deserve being applauded. There are also those that should be researched such as the Mars family. A side note: A friend, unintentionally overheard his mother-in-law and wife discussing whether or not he deserved a raise. He heard his mother-in-law say, "So where is he going to go if we don't give him a raise?" Six months later, divorced and with resume in hand, he began interviewing with all non-family managed firms.

I am the Leader and Never Forget It! If you are into branding, join this leader's herd.

The Story Teller. We have all experienced this leader. Try to make a point or share an experience and this person has a better one. Relaters tend to be the most patient with this person and can usually meet story for story. The Planner agonizes over how many times this story has been told and sometimes out of frustration will finish the story. This approach usually results in another story. If you want to cut this person off, be sure you have an Adventurer and Builder present.

King or Queen of the Buzz Words. Have some fun and make up some nonsense buzz words. The only problem with this approach is they may be added to the list.

One Up-man-ship. "Been there, done that and better." Draw upon your Planner patience. Line up the Adventurers as they will have little patience for this approach. Their quick wit can be a weapon.

Made It to the Top and Forgot Everything Along the Way. Whatever it takes, be it conspiracy or open confrontation, drag this person back down into the trenches. Suggest a day of swapping roles or responsibilities in an effort to build team appreciation. If you are successful, it will be an eye opener for all participants. Every time we suggested this in a particular educational institution, the head administrator had a conflict and was absent. After three attempts we set it up for a fourth time. We gave the administrator the date. We then checked his calendar. Upon his return two days later, we explained the exercise had been cancelled but was going forward that day. We finally had a captive audience. We won't claim a total about face, but we did find him to be more empathic in future dealings.

Acquired a University Degree and Stopped Learning. In all probability you will not change this situation. All you can do is cite and or incorporate current sources where they are needed. Don't be surprised when you hear these sources being cited by this person. Just hope such citations are accurate.

The Socializer. Don't put these types down. Attend the occasional picnic. Remember they are seeking harmony in the workplace.

Keep Them Down on the Farm. Coffee breaks turned into fifteen minute meetings and lunch at your desk are choices. If you accept this environment, then no complaining. If you opt to resist, go through proper channels. Update your resume.

An acquaintance chose to accept this treatment. When asked why, she replied, "Well, on the other side of the coin, he gives out large gift certificates, theatre tickets and weekend retreats at resorts. I know he does it to balance the books. I choose to accept."

The Prince or Princess of Platitudes. "You don't have to work longer hours, just work smarter." Find the wisdom in this platitude. Bring up all colors and start collecting your own platitudes. The Adventurers will enjoy being the delivery system followed by the other colors.

In Charge of Hindsight. Prepare your own Templates. Put the Relaters and Planners in charge.

Goodnik The description of the Goodnik says it all: Defers all confrontations or correctives to second in command or support staff. No trace of fingerprints will be found at the scene, but all know whom the glove fits.

Master of Unfair Play. Any questioning of this person's ideas or contributions is viewed as a threat. This type responds with personal insults. Wisely, he or she usually targets a Planner or Relater. Pull up your Brown and Red. Acknowledge the insult. "What you just said was intended to be hurtful/personal and it did hurt/was personal. But it has nothing to do with what we are talking about---so can we move on to the business at hand?" If you tolerate unfair play you are setting a precedent.

Master or Mistress of Gotcha. The best defense to this approach is a well-planned offence. Become your own quality control. Take a few minutes at the end of each day to journal. Use the format on the following page or create your own. Your journal becomes your resource.

The following journaling idea comes from Dr. Gary Phillips, author of <u>63 Ways of Improving Classroom Instruction</u> and <u>Classroom Rituals for At-Risk-Learners.</u>

1. What was your 5***** win for the day?
   (5 star performance) "If we don't celebrate our successes we are doomed to repeat our failures."

2. What was the most perplexing problem you faced yesterday?
   Our struggles give life meaning. If we don't have a problem, we create one.
   Choosing our struggles wisely is the beginning of leadership and taking control.

3. What was the most prevailing feeling or emotion for the day?
   "93% of the message is emotion."

4. What new idea or learning did you gain yesterday?
   "The best teachers are learners and the best learners are teachers." Resolved: To learn one thing everyday worth remembering for a lifetime.

5. The most challenging activity I faced.
   A job that stretched me out of my comfort zone. "A failure a day keeps complacency away. . . and arrogance too." Challenge = A first time activity or unfamiliar or insufficient skills.

6. My vision for today.
   Best I can imagine for today.

7. More of . . . Less of . . . Ritual
   Today I vow to do more of _____ but less of _____ as a way of enriching my personal life.

8. My affirmation for today.
   What is my "self-talk" about the challenges of today?) Affirm hope, pride, enthusiasm in a daily message to yourself. Mobilize your intuitive side.

9. Predict and Prevent
   One thing that could go wrong today that I could prevent with planning or exploit to my benefit if it's inevitable.

10. A question for which I'd like an answer or something I will do for myself today.

On a Personal Level

In "A Bad Dream or a Nightmare" the leadership types were placed in the work environment. You know from experience, they are also in your personal life. Go through the following list and when applicable fill in the name, be it a friend, spouse, significant other, child, relative, neighbor etc. and the situation. Then write out your strategy and identify the color or colors you need to put into action. Have some fun while at the same time taking control.

Feel free to add your own examples.

> **The Usurper.** Takes credit for all contributions. You put the entire yard into shape. He waters. A neighbor comments on how great it looks. His response, "It took a lot of work!" Don't wait around to be acknowledged. It won't happen.
>
> My husband
>
> **My Strategy:** Pull up my brown builder, speak out and take credit

Feel free to add your own examples.

- **The Usurper.** Takes credit for all contributions.

    My Strategy:_____

- **Poison Pen.** Positive comments are a waste of time.

    My Strategy:_____

- **Emotionally Attached.** My way or the highway.

    My Strategy:_____

- **A Little Knowledge is a Dangerous Thing.** Claims expertise in everything. It doesn't matter whether the information is obscure, out of date or not applicable.

    My Strategy:_____

- ❏ **Throw It Against the Wall.** Quantity not quality is the driving force.

    My Strategy:_____
    _____

- ❏ **The Nitpicker.** Nothing goes unscathed.

    My Strategy:_____
    _____

- ❏ **We and They.** If you agree with me, you are on the "we" team.

    My Strategy:_____
    _____

- ❏ **A Boiling Caldron.** Lets you know through body language and tone of voice that you are in the presence of an impending uncontrollable explosion. If you just go along, the volcano will continue to rest quietly just beneath the surface.

    My Strategy:_____
    _____

- ❏ **Challenge My Ideas, You Challenge Me.** Enough said.

    My Strategy:_____
    _____

- ❏ **Memo Master #1.** Papers the house and counter top with post-a-notes and To-Do lists. Considers them decrees not open to discussion. Great way to ruin a day.
    My Strategy:_____
    _____

- ❏ **Memo Master #2.** Papers the house and counter top with post-a-notes. The message: You are incapable of functioning on your own.

    My Strategy:_____
    _____

- **The Meeting Addict.** Thrives on a committee. Holds meetings whether they are necessary or not.

    My Strategy:_____

- **If You Can't Be Seen, You Must Not Be Working.** Like a watch dog on guard duty he or she hovers continually. Hangs over your shoulder monitoring your every move.

    My Strategy:_____

- **Public Relations.** Total focus is image. The best house, the best car, and the perfect family are on the must list. Intangibles like emotions and feelings take a back seat.

    My Strategy:_____

- **Defers all Decisions.** "Ask your Mother." "Ask your Father." "Ask the dog." Wants a clean slate.

    My Strategy:_____

- **Won't Risk.** All responses begin with "But, what if . . ."

    My Strategy:_____

- **Just One Big Family.** The family that works together, plays together. Individual acts like skiing with friends on the weekend are viewed as mutiny. Can become a smothering situation.

    My Strategy:_____

- **I Am the Leader and Never Forget It!** As if you could. Individuality, respect and independence are not fostered.

    My Strategy:_____

- **The Story Teller.** Lives in the past. Believes the "kids" of today lack the work ethic. Guaranteed to drive off children followed by spouses and friends.

  My Strategy:_____
  _____

- **King or Queen of the Buzz Words.** New buzzwords or phrases will be used like a buzz saw. (acronyms) Kids often use such words to speak in code.

  My Strategy:_____
  _____

- **One Up-man-ship.** Any ideas new ideas or innovations are greeted with, "Been there, done that and better." Quells creativity.

  My Strategy:_____
  _____

- **Made It to the Top and Forgot Everything Along the Way.** Talks the talk of having risen out of the trenches, but has no recall or empathy for anyone else's journey.

  My Strategy:_____
  _____

- **Acquired a University Degree and Stopped Learning.** Hasn't read a professional journal or current text in the last 10-15 years. When challenged, always cites out of date experts.

  My Strategy:_____
  _____

- **The Socializer.** Believes everyone should not only work together, but also socialize together. You just want to raise enough money to pay for new playground equipment.

  My Strategy:_____
  _____

- **Keep Them Down on the Farm.** " I didn't go to college and I made it." "My mother didn't work."

  My Strategy:_____
  _____

- **The Prince or Princess of Platitudes.** "You don't have to work longer hours, just work smarter." "Do more with less." "No pain, no gain."

  My Strategy:_____
  _____

- **In Charge of Hindsight.** Imposes the template of hindsight on any decision that does not pan out 100%.

  My Strategy:_____
  _____

- **Master or Mistress of Gotcha.** You come home and before you have even taken off your coat you find yourself being interrogated. This person either does not comprehend the need for transition time or chooses to disregard it completely.

  My Strategy:_____
  _____

- **The Attacker.** Considers his or her contributions or ideas are inviolate. You suggest the need for reconsideration. You find yourself the target of personal attack.

  My Strategy:_____
  _____

- **Goodnik.** Defers all confrontations or correctives to you.

  My Strategy:_____
  _____

Can you think of any other styles?

- _____

  My Strategy:_____
  _____

A Time to Follow, A Time to Lead, A Time to be Interdependent
The Basis for Team Building

An ancient riddle asked what walked upon four in the morning, upon two at noon and upon three at dusk? The answer is man. In the morning of his life as a baby he crawled dependent upon others for his care. In the noon of his life he walked upon two independent of others. At dusk he walked upon two interdependent upon a cane.

With maturity you have become less dependent with more independent actions on your part. Experience has taught you that a person can never do just one thing. Spray a gallon of pesticide and you impact the entire ecological chain. Disenfranchise another human and the ripple moves across the pond of humanity. At times we try to maintain our position, even to our disadvantage. Consider the leaders who clout their way through a meeting with a set agenda. Anyone who differs is viewed as an adversary. There are team members who participate with hidden agendas. There will also be those frustrated at what they perceive has been a directed outcome with little or no input who will seek to torpedo the final decision. Why? They lack maturity and a willingness to be a part of the whole. In these situations we may stand to gain more if we consider our differences.

Whether you are in the role of a leader or a team player, a mature person must recognize listening involves patience, a desire to understand and openness. You need to be empathetic, courageous and willing to risk intellectually. You must also be willing to let go of your emotional attachments to that which you know. This letting go process requires a shifting of paradigms on your part. Paradigms are how we see our world, not visually but based upon our perceptions, our understandings and our interpretations. A classic example of this would be six witnesses to a crime, each having a different perception of what took place through the filter of their own life experiences.

Being emotionally attached to a position or an idea is normal. The key is, if you are emotionally mature, you will set aside your need to defend and protect your position and be a gatherer. As a gatherer, you will not be so emotionally attached that you reject other viable options. Those options may be better than yours or they may enhance your position. A wise leader and a team member both recognize they are interdependent and a part of the whole. Both know they must be mutually respectful of each other and authentic if effective communication is to take place.

TEAMS, DO YOUR BEST!

The best of team scenarios would involve persons with a commitment to the concept of collectively exchanging ideas in order to reach a best solution to the problem or concern on the table.

A commitment by each of the participants would likely make progress toward such a solution. However, the everyday workplace problem for handling by a team contains very predictable and routine difficulties. We sometimes refer to them as personal agendas, lack of enthusiasm for the concern, personalities that dominate, personal insecurities of participants, knowledge of and wish to conform to the agenda of the highest manager in attendance, reluctance to commit, fear of follow-up blame, or wanting to be a team player without personal risk. See the "Identifying Your Leadership and Team Strengths" on the next page.

Identifying Your Leadership and Team Strengths

Power Chart

Strengths	Builder	Relater	Planner	Adventurer
Prospecting and appointments	★	★		★
Planning and preparation	★		★	
Greeting and meeting		★		
Study and analyzing			★	
Proposal	★			★
Close	★			★
Follow-up and Service		★	★	

A significant part of our involvement is, however, who we are. Our past is with us in our dominant strengths as Builders, Relaters, Planners or Adventurers. It is the one item on the list of variables that is predictable, understandable, and to be used to our advantage in exploring the concern and making positive progress.

It supports a positive involvement when each of us can display and use our strengths. To appreciate and use the strengths of others is to confidently expect the best of the team.

The value of understanding and using behavioral strengths is that there is no secret. The effectiveness of the concept is in knowing each other. For the team leader, the idea has always been to "know your people". The concept of behavioral identification shows us how to "know your people". It is equally valuable for the team members to know each other as well as the leader.

We do not usually have the luxury of selecting a team with a perfect balance of behavioral strengths from a small group. We do, however, have the advantage of identifying our weaknesses. A team with five strong Builders has the behavioral identification tools for recognizing that any decision they make will reflect that Builder strength. They would also have the obligation to recognize that their work will be missing the strengths of the other colors. They should anticipate and appreciate the probable ideas of the Relaters, Adventurers and Planners who are not in attendance.

Another alternative if your team is not balanced: consider asking team members to assume the role of missing or weak colors. Use the cards as reminders. Place the colored card in front of the team member who accepts the responsibility for representing that color.

This is not a natural process for the five Builders. It is a learned process requiring practice and attention. Without planning and careful attention by the Builders on this team, they will not value the detailed investigative and thoughtful process the Planner finds necessary. Without that attention, they would not consider the impact their plan/decision would have on Relaters or Adventurers.

Teamwork is valuable for a variety of good reasons. Why not get the most out of it?

Whether you are in the role of leadership or team player, an understanding of Winning Colors® gives you an edge. It serves as a tool for understanding team members, family and peers. It provides you with the basis for knowing and anticipating positions and communication styles based on behavioral strengths.

As a Planner, use your strength for consideration of detail and risk intellectually by your example.
As a Relater, do what you do best, bringing people together in an atmosphere of mutual respect.
As an Adventurer, use your natural bent for risk, your ability to cut to the core and generate enthusiasm.
As a Builder, keep the group focused on the task and provide the structure that progresses in a direct line to the goal.

*The significant problems we face cannot be solved at the same
Level of thinking we were at when we created them.*
---Albert Einstein

"When we restrict our level of awareness, our universe stops expanding. If we are emotionally attached to the concept that our way is correct, logical, reasonable and practical we will tend to surround ourselves with those who are like us if we wish to avoid conflict. Creativeness and ideas will be restricted. Our rainbow will contain only one color.

Raise our level of awareness, seek to understand and value the behavioral strengths of others and our universe comes to life and begins expanding.

Several years ago this writer had the opportunity to stand for the first time at the base of the longest falls in western Canada. As long as I live I will remember the beauty of those falls and the message of that setting. As I looked up I saw a rainbow erupting out of the falls. As I followed its course looking for the pot of gold, I found it in the form of a magnificent rugged fir, well over 150 feet in height growing out of a sheer wall of slate. More than half of its roots were tenaciously attached like webbing to the outer surface of the rock. Its branches were continuously being pounded by the spray of the falls and whipped by the accompanying wind. And yet there it had chosen against all odds to protest, fight and grow in no one's shadow. It was a superb example of conflict in nature. We can all be like that magnificent fir if we choose to let our roots be like silken steel, are aware of our environment, bend with the wind when necessary and reach for the sky with our branches. When we do so, the rainbow will thread its way through our branches." [6]

**The four elements
Fire, Water, Air and Earth
The dance continues . . .**
---*Shay*

*Perhaps
the most important thing
is to face ourselves
in the mirror and
to color ourselves
the colors of
our choice.*

*If
only one color
was correct,
we would never see
the beauty of the rainbow.*

Shay Thoelke

Footnotes

[1] Stefan Neilson and Shay Thoelke, <u>Leadership, Team Building, Conflict Resolution, Self-esteem</u> (Seattle: Aeon Hierophant, Revised 2001).

Stefan Neilson, <u>Communication</u> (Seattle: Aeon Hierophant, 1998) 5, 9-11.

[2] Stefan Neilson and Shay Thoelke, <u>Careers Unlimited To Be or Not To Be</u> (Seattle: Aeon Hierophant, 1999) 79-87.

[3] Neilson and Thoelke, 101-110.

[4] Neilson and Thoelke, 89-98.

[5] Neilson and Thoelke, 112-122.

[6] Stefan Neilson and Shay Thoelke, <u>Conflict Resolution Through Winning Colors</u> (Seattle: Aeon Hierophant, 1999) 228.

Maximize your communication power with the following texts

Conflict Resolution Through Winning Colors®, (the key to understanding and preventing violent behavior) is a unique present behavioral observation tool. Present behavioral identification is crucial for violence prevention. Many conflict resolution programs ignore this basic premise. **Winning Colors®** is simple to understand and apply. Yet this workable process for resolving personal differences is profound in implication. In a matter of seconds the behavioral make-up of those in conflict, the basis for solving any discord and preventing violence is revealed. Application strategies for resolving conflicts, which lead to violence, are given, rather than theory. What makes this text unique is that it may be used on an individual basis, in support groups or with large groups or classes.

Careers Unlimited: To Be or Not to Be Through the Winning Colors® Process matches your present behaviors to those demanded by job descriptions. This is the ultimate career identification guide. None if any inventories identify the behaviors crucial to job success and personal satisfaction as does the Winning Colors® process. This powerful step out of the ordinary includes multiple exercises and a set of communication identification cards.

In the student friendly ***Winning Colors® video,*** four youths in conflict become a powerful creative team through the Winning Colors® process. In part two of the video a hostage negotiator discusses how the Winning Colors® process may be applied in conflict hostile situations. The video is applicable to university, college, high school and middle school.

Energizing The Internet of the Brain. Finally, there is a book of energizers for adults, university, college and high school students. What makes the energizers unique is they not only activate the participant physically, but also serve to engage the brain. This text is available in coil and hard bound.

Leadership, Team Building, Self-esteem, Conflict Resolution, Communication manual is a condensed guide of the Winning Colors® process, a whole person approach to personal development in contrast to type casting and pigeon holing. It is a powerful behavioral observation tool and not an assessment. It can be used as a complete guide for presenting the Winning Colors® process in seminars, presentations and employee training as well as a participant's manual. The Winning Colors process is based on the proven research of the behavioral paradigm: Identify and measure behaviors, apply a treatment or plan of action and measure the resulting behavioral change. Present behavioral founded communication is indicated by a unique card sort and pen and pencil procedure. Includes a set of communication identification cards.

Here's Looking at You Kid! is an instructor's manual for the Winning Colors® process with kindergarten and elementary students. A 120 page manual which contains lesson plans for a 24-48 week program using multi-sensory techniques for developing basic English skills in conjunction with positive communication behaviors. It identifies a young person's present behaviors in a self-esteeming format for their communication development.

Hands-on instructor manuals and cards are available for all ages. Canadian youth and adult manuals and cards as well as Spanish cards are available. Please contact us for a catalog. The cards indicate present behaviors, motivation and self-esteem.

Looking for Materials That Will Meet The Needs of an Individual Student or an Entire Class Fulfilling a Community Services Requirement?

Service Learning A Community Team Experience Using Winning Colors® In an Elementary School ©2001 by Shay contains materials to be used by student mentors when working with grades 1-5.

Service Learning A Community Team Experience Using Winning Colors® In A Middle School Level Two ©2001 by Shay contains materials to be used by student mentors when working with middle school students.

Service Learning A Community Team Experience Using Winning Colors® Level Three ©2001 by Shay contains materials to be used with teenagers or adults. Level Three workbook supports a Senior project or Community Services Graduation Requirement. Currently many states require 45 hours for 1/2 credit and 90 hours for a full credit. This program provides sufficient activities to meet such a requirement for an individual or group of students.

Aeon Communications, Inc.,
P.O.Box 96, Mountlake Terrace, WA 98043
(425) 672-8222 fax (425) 672-9777 e-mail: winningcolors@mindspring.com
website: winningcolors.com